READING GROUP CHOICES
2008

Selections for lively book discussions

Published in the United States by Reading Group Choices,
a division of Connxsys LLC

ISBN: (13) 978-0-9759742-3-0
ISBN: (10) 0-9759742-3-8

For further information, contact:
Barbara Drummond Mead
Reading Group Choices
532 Cross Creek Court
Chester, MD 21619
Toll-free: 1-866-643-6883
info@ReadingGroupChoices.com
www.ReadingGroupChoices.com

Welcome to

READING GROUP Choices

Selecting Discussible Books Since 1995

From every book invisible threads reach out to other books; and as the mind comes to use and control those threads the whole panorama of the world's life, past and present, becomes constantly more varied and interesting, while at the same time the mind's own powers of reflection and judgment are exercised and strengthened.

—Helen E. Haines

Reading groups epitomize and enhance this sentiment. By bringing together minds that are diverse, yet similar, to discuss and reflect the ideas and philosophies of writers, reading groups expand their knowledge and understanding of themselves and the world. Books are teachers and friends that don't judge, punish, or scorn. The lessons are the authors' and the readers' collective understanding of ideas written down.

In *Reading Group Choices 2008*, fiction and nonfiction illuminate the many threads of life. The historical and cultural differences of countries, and stories of countries split by ideology, religion, and/or greed, open avenues for something new and unknown. The joys and sorrows of love, relationships, and family lead members of the group to discuss their own lives. The writing and sharing of life stories, as in memoirs, offer minimalist sketches that may lead to a discovery of the many universal truths.

"We read to know we are not alone," said C. S. Lewis. We hope this collection leads you and your group to better and wider understanding of "the whole panorama of the world's life, past and present . . . "

—BARBARA AND CHARLIE MEAD

AUTHORS WANT TO ANSWER YOUR QUESTIONS!

Look for this symbol and your reading group may schedule a conversation with the author.

For an opportunity to have a lively discussion with an author, please register at

www.ReadingGroupChoices.com

Scheduling begins in December 2007.
Author Conversations will be scheduled for 2008.

Author Conversations are Easy and Fun!

All your group needs is to read the book, have a speaker phone, and let the chat begin!

Tips for a successful author conversations:

- Schedule a **Reading Group Choices**' author by registering at www.ReadingGroupChoices.com
- Have your group read the book – **very important.**
- Meet at least 30 minutes before the conversation to prepare questions for the author. Use questions from *Reading Group Choices* and other sources, as well as your own.
- Have an order of questions to prevent two or more people talking at once (very confusing for the author).
- Have everyone get a chance to speak to avoid one member dominating the conversation.
- Have members say their first names before asking a question of the author; this gives the author a feeling of personal connection even though the chat is on the phone.

Have a fun and lively conversation!

CONTENTS

Early in 2007, we asked thousands of book groups to tell us what books they read and discussed during the previous year that they enjoyed most. The top ten titles were:

1. *The Kite Runner* by Khaled Hosseini (Riverhead)
2. *My Sister's Keeper* by Jodi Picoult (Washington Street Press)
3. *The Memory Keeper's Daughter* by Kim Edwards (Penguin Books)
4. *The Glass Castle* by Jeannette Walls (Scribner Book Company).
5. S*now Flower and the Secret Fan* by Lisa See (Random House Trade)
6. *The Devil in the White City: Murder, Magic and Madness and the Fair That Changed America* (Illinois) by Erik Larson (Vintage)
7. *The Curious Incident of the Dog in the Night-time* by Mark Haddon (Vintage)
8. TIE: *March* by *Geraldine Brooks* (Penguin Books) and *The History Of Love* by Nicole Krauss (W. W. Norton)
9. TIE: *Red Tent* by Anita Diamant (Picador) and *Pope Joan* by Donna Woolfolk Cross (Ballantine Books)
10. TIE: *Year of Wonders* by Geraldine Brooks (Penguin Books) and *Water for Elephants* by Sara Gruen (Algonquin Books of Chapel Hill)

ABUNDANCE
A Novel of Marie Antoinette

AUTHOR: **Sena Jeter Naslund**

PUBLISHER: Harper Perennial, June 2007

WEBSITE: www.senajeternaslund.com
www.harpercollins.com

AVAILABLE IN:
Paperback, 592 pages, $15.95
ISBN: 978-0-06-082540-9

SUBJECT: Biography/History/Women's Lives (Fiction)

"Enchanting. . . . Opulent and fabulous, as encrusted with detail as one of Marie's shimmering dresses . . . a complete page turner. Grade: A."
—Entertainment Weekly

"If you read one book about Marie Antoinette, let it be Sena Jeter Naslund's gripping, gabby, and beautifully poignant novel. Naslund's writing is sumptuous and personal, and she manages to make that most of remote subjects—an eighteenth-century queen—relevant to modern times. You know how her story ends. But the journey is so abundant with joy, grief, and all those ordinary events that make up our lives, you'll lose your head reading about it." —USA Today

SUMMARY: Far from her family, her country, and her home and thrust into the role of woman, wife, and queen at the age of 14, Marie Antoinette lived a brief but astonishing existence. With searing insight and wondrous narrative skill, Sena Jeter Naslund offers a fresh, vivid picture of this compelling woman that goes beyond popular myth. Based on impeccable historical research, *Abundance* reveals a young woman very different from the one who supposedly said of the starving French peasants, "Let them eat cake."

ABOUT THE AUTHOR: **Sena Jeter Naslund** is writer in residence at the University of Louisville, program director of the Spalding University brief-residency MFA in Writing, and current Kentucky Poet Laureate. Recipient of the Harper Lee Award and the Southeastern Library Association Fiction Award, she is cofounder of *The Louisville Review* and the *Fleur-de-Lis Press*. She lives in Louisville, Kentucky.

1. Sena Jeter Naslund has divided her novel into five "acts," like a Shakespearean play. Does Marie Antoinette achieve the stature of a tragic protagonist at the end of the novel?

2. Recount the dramatic evolution of Marie Antoinette's character, from her arrival in France at the age of 14 to her death just shy of 38. What prompts Marie Antoinette's transformation from callow moralist and pliant dauphine in early chapters to empathetic mother and brave stoic in the novel's culmination at the Conciergerie?

3. From her arrival at Versailles as a girl, Marie Antoinette exists in a perpetual state of enclosure. Discuss Naslund's extended treatment of this idea. Is Marie Antoinette's life in France tantamount to that of the proverbial bird in the gilded cage?

4. Revisit the pivotal last chapter of "Act Four," which renders the eruption of revolution in stark counterpoint to the queen's blissful, penultimate encounter with Fersen. In particular, consider Marie Antoinette's poignant musings on the revolutionaries' freshly-coined slogan, "liberté, equalité, fraternité." What do these words mean to Marie Antoinette?

5. Discuss the interconnectedness of female identity and performance in *Abundance*. What does it mean, for instance, that Marie Antoinette feels most engaged and alive when she is playing a role on the stage?

6. How does the texture of this identity/performance theme shift once Marie Antoinette is faced with the prospect of fleeing? To flee, in Marie Antoinette's estimation, is to abandon her "role."

7. In what specific ways has Naslund's rendering of late-18th-century France come to inform, challenge, or even contradict altogether your previous understandings of the particular cause of the French Reign of Terror?

8. How do Naslund's references to and subtle demonstrations of prevailing philosophies of the day—including the outmoded optimism of Gottfried-Leibniz; the measured, conservative skepticism of David Hume; the proto-civil libertarianism of the secular Voltaire; and the revolutionary ideas of Jean-Jacques Rousseau—color and shape the novel's inexorable march toward the Reign of Terror?

9. What kind of a man does Louis-Auguste become? And what kind of king?

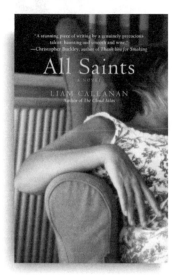

ALL SAINTS

AUTHOR: *Liam Callanan*

PUBLISHER: Dial Press, April 2008

WEBSITE: www.dialpress.com
www.liamcallanan.com

AVAILABLE IN:
Paperback, 288 pages, $12.00
ISBN: (13) 978-0-385-33697-0
ISBN: (10) 0-385-33697-7

SUBJECT: Faith/Relationships/Personal Challenges (Fiction)

"All Saints *asks a very private question: How do you move forward in life when faced with your own failures? . . . The desires of the soul, the impulses of the flesh and the confines of the human condition drive the novel's story until the line dividing the saints from the sinners is blurred."*
—*Los Angeles Times*

"All Saints *is a jewel of a book: bright, sharp-witted, full of the fantastical lore of the saints and the secret yearnings of everyday American life, full of secrets and surprises."* —**Dan Chaon, author of *You Remind Me of Me***

SUMMARY: By life's midpoint Emily has seen three husbands, dozens of friends, and hundreds of students come and go. And now her classroom, long her refuge, is proving to be anything but. Though her popular, occasionally irreverent church history course is rich with stories of long-dead saints, Emily uneasily discovers that it's her own tumultuous life that fascinates certain students most. She in turn finds herself drawn into their world, their secrets, and the fateful choices they make. A novel of mystery and illumination, calling and choice, *All Saints* explores lives lived in a fragile sanctuary—from Emily and her many saints to a priest facing his own mortality and a teenager tormented by desire. Told with grace and compassion, this is a spellbinding novel of provocative storytelling.

ABOUT THE AUTHOR: **Liam Callanan** is the author of *The Cloud Atlas*, which was an Edgar Award finalist for best first novel. A frequent public radio essayist, his work has also appeared in *The New York Times Book Review, Slate, Good Housekeeping*, and elsewhere. He teaches at the University of Wisconsin—Milwaukee.

1. How did it affect your reading to know that a male author had created Emily, a pitch-perfect female narrator? How would you characterize the way she sees the world?

2. What was your initial understanding of Emily's revelation that she had kissed a boy, for the first time in her life, at age fifty? How did your impressions of her shift as her marriage history unfolded?

3. Discuss the irony of Emily's classroom topics. How do the students' oral reports, and the concept of saints and popes, contrast with the circumstances of modern life presented in the novel? How do you define "saint"?

4. What do the two coasts—New York and California—mean to Emily? How does she perceive the cultural differences and landscapes of these two settings? What types of dividing lines are created between the novel's two parts, Fall and Spring?

5. Were any of your teachers like Emily? Did Edgar, Cecily, and Paul remind you of any of your high-school classmates? What makes *All Saints* both an unusual and a very typical high school?

6. What comfort does Emily derive from Mrs. Ramirez? How does it compare to the comfort she derives from going to church, and in particular from being Catholic? Share your own experiences with mystery and faith.

7. Discuss the notion of secrecy that permeates many of the characters in *All Saints*. Is secrecy a form of dishonesty? What role does confession (informal and otherwise) play in the novel? What does Paul's essay reveal in chapter nine?

8. Should Martin have had to take a vow of celibacy at all? Discuss the various temptations confronted by the characters in the novel.

9. What do you predict for Emily's future? What does *All Saints* ultimately say about the cycles of birth and death?

10. What aspects of courage does the author paint in *All Saints*? How are heroism and humanity presented in this novel?

11. Discuss the nature of belief in *All Saints*. Not just spiritual belief, but also the belief people have in each other, and in the concepts of friendship, love, commitment, and forgiveness?

ASTRID AND VERONIKA

AUTHOR: *Linda Olsson*

PUBLISHER: Penguin Books, February 2007

WEBSITE: us.penguingroup.com
www.lindaolsson.net

AVAILABLE IN:
Paperback, 288 pages, $14.00
ISBN: (13) 978-0-14-303807-8
ISBN: (10) 0-14-303807-9

SUBJECT: Relationships/Women's
Lives/Family (Fiction)

"Linda Olsson's first novel casts the themes of secrecy, passion and loss in the shape of a double helix, intertwining the stories of two women, one young and one nearing the end of life, around the axis of their unlikely friendship." —**The New York Times**

"Linda Olsson evokes, with great beauty and precision, the landscape of a friendship between two very different women, each caught in a tragic moment from the past. Their connection, initially as tentative and fragile as the first filaments of ice, gradually strengthens, allowing each woman to give voice to her stories, and in doing so to reclaim 'a heart for beauty.' Subtle, penetrating, and beautifully written, Astrid and Veronika *affirms the power of narrative to transform."*—**Kim Edwards, author of** *The Memory Keeper's Daughter*

SUMMARY: With extraordinary emotional power, Linda Olsson's stunningly well-crafted debut novel recounts the unusual and unexpected friendship that develops between two women. Veronika, a young writer from New Zealand, rents a house in a small Swedish village as she tries to come to terms with a recent tragedy while also finishing a novel. Her arrival is silently observed by Astrid, an older, reclusive neighbor who slowly becomes a presence in Veronika's life, offering comfort in the form of companionship and lovingly prepared home-cooked meals. Set against a haunting Swedish landscape, *Astrid & Veronika* is a lyrical and meditative novel of love and loss.

ABOUT THE AUTHOR: **Linda Olsson** was born in Stockholm, Sweden. She has lived in Kenya, Singapore, Britain, and Japan. *Astrid and Veronika* is her first novel.

1. Astrid has been solitary for so long. Why, then, do you think she is drawn to Veronika, essentially a stranger, and then later allows herself to open up to her so freely?

2. The houses in the novel serve almost as characters. Discuss how the author uses the houses in the novel. What is the importance of a home in our lives? How does our house/living space define us? What do you think your house/living space says about you?

3. Astrid's mother committed suicide when Astrid was six-years-old; Veronika's mother left when Veronika was a child. Talk about the theme of the "absent mother" and how it influences these characters' lives.

4. What did you think of Astrid's confession regarding the death of her child? Were you able to understand her actions? Did knowing this about her past affect the way you felt about her? What do you think Astrid expected Veronika's reaction would be to her story? Was Astrid taking a risk in telling her? Why do you think Veronika reacts in the way she does?

5. Veronika feels very guilty about the death of her fiancé and agonizes over what she could have done differently that day to prevent his death. Why do you think she feels so guilty?

6. When Astrid tries on the floral swimsuit during Veronika's birthday "outing," the women burst out into laughter. (p. 85). Why do the women find this moment so hysterically funny? How does this day, Veronika's birthday, serve as a turning point in the novel?

7. After her husband dies, Astrid says to Veronika , "There was nothing more to be afraid of. . . . It was never about him. It was about me" (p.167). What does she mean?

8. Veronika visits her father after her fiancé's death, and when she is leaving her father begins to say, "I wish . . ." but doesn't complete the sentence (p. 200). What do you think he was going to say? How would you describe Veronika's relationship with him?

9. Great literary novels skillfully incorporate sometimes elaborate symbolism. In *Astrid & Veronika*, Olsson makes repeated and significant references to water. Discuss the symbolic function of water in the novel and consider how water may be connected with Olsson's major themes.

10. Discuss how the seasons shape the novel. How do the seasons influence the characters? Discuss the ways that the seasons affect you throughout the year? Are your memories connected to the seasons in which they took place?

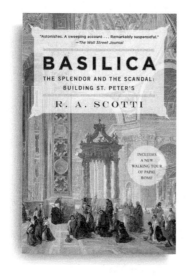

BASILICA
The Splendor and the Scandal: Building St. Peter's

AUTHOR: *R. A. Scotti*

PUBLISHER: Plume, May 2007

WEBSITE: www.penguin.com
www.rascotti.com

AVAILABLE IN:
Paperback, 336 pages, $15.00
ISBN: (13) 978-0-452-28860-7
ISBN: (10) 0452288607

SUBJECT: History/Art (Nonfiction)

"Fascinating history reveals how the world's most glorious house of worship emerged from decades of trial and scandal. A riveting portrait of the papacy, complete with its triumphs, intrigue, and excesses."
—**Kirkus Reviews**

"Tells the story of the building of St. Peter's—and the history of a turbulent century—in the most entertaining and enlightening way." —**Ross King, author of** *Brunelleschi's Dome*

"A fascinating tale of genius, power, and money." —**Publishers Weekly**

SUMMARY: Covering nearly four acres and soaring 425 feet at its highest point, St. Peter's Basilica is both a monument to the glory of God and a testament to the genius, ambition, and will of men. R. A. Scotti's *Basilica* chronicles the epic construction effort behind this architectural treasure. Propelled by artistic inspiration, social upheaval, and political intrigue, the story spans two centuries and includes larger-than-life characters.

ABOUT THE AUTHOR: **R. A. Scotti** is the author of six previous books, including several espionage novels and, most recently, the best-selling *Sudden Sea: The Great Hurricane of 1938*. She lives in New York City with her family.

1. The outrage sparked by the demolition of Constantine's basilica to make way for the new St. Peter's brings to mind modern battles between real estate developers and defenders of historic landmarks. And yet today, the "new" basilica is itself a historic treasure—one of the architectural marvels of the late Renaissance. To what degree do you believe a city's architectural legacy should be preserved? Where do we draw the line between preserving the past and embracing the future?

2. Before reading *Basilica*, how aware were you of Renaissance-era papal practices, such as the selling of indulgences and venal offices, or of the questionable moral character of the era's popes? Does the Vatican's checkered history affect your perception of the institution today?

3. Scotti writes, "Religion is illusion . . . and the gleam of gold, the clouds of incense, . . . the sacred art and evocative music, create that illusion. Stripped bare of all but its dogma, it would be exponentially reduced." Do you agree?

4. Scotti details the vast sums spent on the basilica at a time when most Catholics lived in abject poverty. Does this allocation of resources seem morally justifiable?

5. Like many monumental structures of antiquity, St. Peter's was built on a scale and with a level of craftsmanship that seems inconceivable today. Are there any architectural achievements of the last century that seem on par with the construction of St. Peter's?

6. Today, the Sistine Chapel ceiling is regarded as one of Michelangelo's greatest achievements. But he saw the commission as a punishment—a distraction from what he considered his most important work: sculpting the tomb of Julius. Do you think Julius's redirection of Michelangelo's talent brought the artist to greater heights? Is there an argument to be made that artists, in general, create better work under direction?

7. The book describes the many personal rivalries and animosities among the artists who worked on the basilica. Do you think the great artists of the Renaissance—or of any era—could have reached the same heights without this competitiveness?

8. Of the many historic figures in *Basilica*—from Julius II to Raphael to Martin Luther—who would you most like to meet? If you could put a question to any one of them, what would it be?

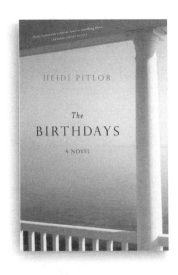

THE BIRTHDAYS

AUTHOR: *Heidi Pitlor*

PUBLISHER: W. W. Norton, June 2007

WEBSITE: www.wwnorton.com

AVAILABLE IN:
Paperback, 368 pages, $13.95
ISBN: (13) 978-0-393-32993-3
ISBN: (10) 0-393-32993-3

SUBJECT: Family/Relationships/Personal Challenges (Fiction)

"In The Birthdays *Heidi Pitlor demonstrates a wonderful sense of setting, plot, and occasion, but what makes this novel so absorbing, and so masterful, is her sense of character. In some magical way Pitlor manages to make us feel what it is like to be both a parent and a child, both old and young, both bitter and hopeful. An exhilarating debut."* —**Margot Livesey, author of** *Banishing Verona*

"Anyone who knows firsthand the modern-day struggles of veering into middle age alongside siblings, in-laws, and elderly parents (and isn't that most of us nowadays?) will find this book captivating, moving, painfully funny, and so very, very true." —**Julie Glass, author of** *Three Junes*

SUMMARY: *The Birthdays* tells the story of a unique family on the brink of a new generation, and examines modern-day marriage, pregnancy, and parenthood. On an island off the coast of Maine, the Miller family reunites to celebrate the father's seventy-fifth birthday. Each of the adult children is expecting his or her own first child. The eldest, Daniel, grapples with the fact that his wife had to be artificially inseminated. Jake, the middle child, discovers that his wife is carrying twins after many years of infertility treatments. Hilary—the free-spirited youngest daughter—arrives in Maine five months pregnant with no identifiable father in sight. Their coming together sets off a series of fireworks, and after the weekend, none of the Millers will emerge the same.

ABOUT THE AUTHOR: **Heidi Pitlor** is a former senior editor at Houghton Mifflin and is the annual series editor for *The Best American Short Stories*. She lives in Boston, Massachusetts.

1. Compare the ways in which the women who have married into the family interact with Ellen and Joe. Why do you think Liz connects with her in-laws, while Brenda doesn't seem to?

2. At one point there is an exchange between MacNeil and Ellen where Ellen says of Daniel, "He could have been a real artist." MacNeil replies, "He is a real artist." Is MacNeil, a relative outsider, able to make a better assessment of Daniel? Does this relate to Ellen's inability to understand what it is exactly that Jake does for a living?

3. What role do age and age differences play in each of the relationships? For example, Brenda is much younger than Daniel—how does this affect the way they relate to each other? How is Ellen's affection for MacNeil, and for Joe, different from the affection expressed between the younger couples?

4. In addition to this, discuss the role of generational differences in the book. How do the parents' expectations for their children affect the children's own wants and goals? To what degree have Ellen's and Joe's philosophies on life rubbed off on their children?

5. Discuss which characters you most identify with and why. Is it easier to feel sympathetic to those whose difficulties are externally caused or accidental (like Daniel) than to those whose situation is largely due to their own choices (like Hilary)?

6. Do you agree with Brenda and Daniel's decision to use an anonymous sperm donor (and artificial insemination)? If you found yourself in a similar situation, would you choose this solution?

7. Likewise, Jake and Liz have gotten pregnant with the help of modern science. Do they seem to have grappled with a moral crisis in making this decision? What do you make of our society's embrace of reproductive technology?

8. Discuss Pitlor's narrative approach. What is the effect of her telling the story told from all the different points of view?

9. Pitlor uses metaphor frequently. Discuss some of the most significant metaphors in *The Birthdays*. For example, does Joe's turtle signify anything? What is the role of the art of Corcoran?

10. Why do you think Pitlor chose to set the book on an island? What role does the setting play? How can setting add to a story?

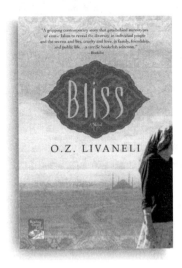

BLISS

AUTHOR: *O. Z. Livaneli*

PUBLISHER: St. Martin's Griffin, September 2007

WEBSITE: www.readinggroupgold.com www.livaneli.net.

AVAILABLE IN:
Paperback, 304 pages, $13.95
ISBN: 978-0-312-36054-2

SUBJECT: Cultural & World Issues/ Women's Lives/Personal Challenges (Fiction)

"A gripping contemporary story that gets behind stereotypes of exotic Islam to reveal the diversity in individual people and the secrets and lies, cruelty and love, in family, friendship, and public life. This will make a terrific bookclub selection. . . . ." —**Booklist**

"Eye-opening and deeply moving—essential for anyone looking for decency in the world today." —**Kirkus Reviews** (**starred review**)

"A compelling premise, set in a part of the world that many American readers are curious about . . . hard to put down" —**The Cleveland Plain Dealer**

SUMMARY: *Bliss* is the story of Meryem, a young village girl who is raped by her uncle. An outcast for shaming her family, she is locked in the cellar and expected to kill herself. When she refuses, her cousin and childhood playmate Cemal is charged with carrying out the honor killing, to "take her to Istanbul" as the village euphemism goes. By chance, their paths cross with Irfan, a professor from Istanbul. Together they embark on a journey that sets them free. Beautifully wrought and simply told, *Bliss* brings attention to the difficult situation of women in Turkey, and captures universal truths forged in the space between people from opposite ends of a complicated culture.

ABOUT THE AUTHOR: **O. Z. Livaneli**, one of Turkey's most prominent authors, is also an accomplished composer, and previously served as an elected member of the Turkish Parliament.

1. Discuss the reasons why the author may have chosen the title *Bliss* for his novel. What is its significance?
2. Did you have any ideas or opinions on Turkey before reading the novel? Take a moment to talk about your collective knowledge of Turkish history and culture before and after reading *Bliss*.
3. Who is your favorite character in *Bliss* and why? Are there those you like who are, in fact, "unlikable?" Take a moment to talk about the cast of characters—and range of personality types—in the novel.
4. Discuss the two distinct settings of the novel—the small rural village and the larger-than-life city. What does each locale mean to each of the main characters?
5. In what ways do Meryem and Cemal's encounters with different people on the train shed light on the problems of identity that characterize contemporary Turkey? Also, in what ways is sailing the Aegean Sea symbolic for them both?
6. What are the themes of tradition and modernity, religion vs. secularity, and male domination and female empowerment that resonate throughout *Bliss*?
7. Each of the main protagonists in Bliss experiences tragedy on a profound, indeed existential level. How would you describe each character's personal transformation? What unites them in their struggle to overcome their demons?
8. How do you interpret Irfan's final resolution at the end of the novel about what kind of a life he's to lead? And what about Meryem's?
9. How would you describe Irfan's relation to Hidayet, a character who never appears in the novel but who's always in Irfan's thoughts?
10. One of the chapters in the novel is titled "At Night Don Quixote, Sancho Panza in the Morning." Were there times in your life when you felt the same?
11. At one point in the novel Irfan likens himself and all Turkish intellectuals to "trapeze flyers." Why?
12. Why is Irfan's relationship with his parents marked with deep feelings of guilt?
13. What are the differences between Irfan's and Cemal's attitudes about national identity and belonging?
14. Discuss the ambassador's comment that there are three phases in the life of an individual: camel phase, lion phase, and childhood phase.
15. There are numerous references to mythical figures and stories in the novel. Why do you think the idea of myth has such an important place in *Bliss*?

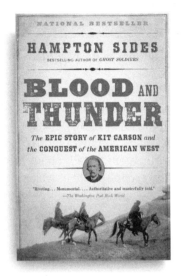

BLOOD AND THUNDER
The Epic Story of Kit Carson and the Conquest of the American West

AUTHOR: *Hampton Sides*

PUBLISHER: Anchor Books, October 2007

WEBSITE: www.ReadingGroupCenter.com
www.bloodandthunderbook.com

AVAILABLE IN:
Paperback, 592 pages, $15.95
ISBN: 978-1-4000-3110-8

SUBJECT: American History/Biography (Nonfiction)

"Riveting. . . . Monumental. . . . Authoritative and masterfully told."
—*The Washington Post Book World*

"The cast of characters is large and the landscape vast. We see a panorama and a whole history, intricately laced with wonder and meaning, coalesce into a story of epic proportions, a story full of authority and color, truth and prophecy, a story that is uniquely ours." —*The New York Times Book Review*

SUMMARY: The author of the bestselling *Ghost Soldiers* returns with the epic chronicle of the real American West. *Blood and Thunder* brings the history of the American conquest of the West to vivid life through the interactions of the three main forces of the territory—American Indians, Mexicans, and Americans—and through the exploits of the legendary Kit Carson. An illiterate mountain man who mastered seven Indian dialects, Carson had more respect for the tribes than did any other American; yet he was also a cold-blooded killer who willingly followed orders tantamount to massacre. Grand in scope, immediate in detail, and fascinating in historical revelation, *Blood and Thunder* is a magnificent portrait of the American West.

ABOUT THE AUTHOR: **Hampton Sides** is editor-at-large for *Outside* magazine and the author of the international bestseller, *Ghost Soldiers*, which was the basis for the 2005 Miramax film, *The Great Raid*. *Ghost Soldiers* won the 2002 PEN USA Award for nonfiction, and Sides's magazine work has been twice nominated for National Magazine Awards for feature writing. He is also the author of *Americana* and *Stomping Grounds*. He lives in New Mexico with his wife, Anne, and their three sons.

1. The contradictions in Kit Carson's personality make him an alluring figure. How was Carson able to embrace so many aspects of Native American culture, even marrying two Indian women, but nonetheless lead campaigns that crippled them? To whom (or what) was he most loyal?

2. How did the post-colonial unrest in Mexico affect U.S attempts to purchase and conquer the West? What racial hierarchies were in place among Hispanic and Indian populations there? What is the current legacy of these conflicts?

3. Is the underlying concept of Manifest Destiny still used to justify violence around the world? What did Carson's words and actions reveal about his understanding of divine will?

4. What does Carson's illiteracy, paired with his knowledge of numerous languages, say about him? What distinguishes the power of the written word from the power of the spoken word, as evidenced by Carson's enthusiasm for an epic poem by Lord Byron? Is a society truly literate if its members are not versed in more than one language?

5. In what way was the landscape a "warrior" in *Blood and Thunder* (as in the Washington Expedition's encounter with Canyon de Chelly, depicted in chapter thirty-four)? How have various populations perceived the landscape of the West, from ancient populations to modern-day tourists?

6. Do Americans still have an emotional investment in believing that the "winning" of the West was a glorious, even heroic endeavor? How does the real story of Western conquest differ from the one we were taught in grade school?

7. During its first war of foreign aggression, the United States seized many thousands of square miles of territory from Mexico. How should this historical fact shape the current debate over Mexican immigration—especially considering that the states most keenly affected by the immigration controversy (California, Arizona, New Mexico, and Texas) are the very states the United States appropriated from Mexico?

For the complete Reading Group Guide,
visit www.ReadingGroupCenter.com.

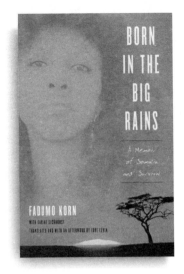

BORN IN THE BIG RAINS
A Memoir of Somalia and Survival

AUTHOR: *Fadumo Korn*

PUBLISHER: The Feminist Press at C.U.N.Y., April 2008

WEBSITE: www.feministpress.org

AVAILABLE IN:
Paperback, 192 pages, $15.95
ISBN: 978-155861578-6

ALSO AVAILABLE IN:
Hardcover, 185 pages, $23.95
ISBN: 978-155861531-1

SUBJECT: Women's Lives/Cultural & World Issues (Memoir)

"A moving, unsentimental, and informative account of the painful personal experience that inspired, and continues to fuel, [Korn's] work."
—**Francine Prose, People Magazine, (starred Critic's Choice)**

"This impassioned, beautifully written memoir is a testament to the possibility of wedding literary prose to sophisticated political arguments . . . a brutally honest, politically sensitive, and bold addition to literature on global women's health." —***Publishers Weekly* (starred review)**

SUMMARY: Korn begins by describing her life as a feisty Somali nomad, freely roaming her country's steppes. She undergoes FGM (female genital mutilation) at the age of seven, and everything changes. She is sent to Mogadishu for treatment of complications, and as civil war looms, finds herself living amid luxury in the capital with an uncle related to the president. Korn escapes the violence that envelops Somalia when she is sent to Europe for advanced medical care. There she finds physical and emotional release from trauma, marries a German, bears a child, and becomes an international anti-FGM activist.

ABOUT THE AUTHOR: **Fadumo Korn** is vice president of FORWARD–Germany, an organization dedicated to promoting action to stop FGM. She lives with her family in Munich.

1. Early in the memoir, Fadumo writes that the status of Somali families increased with the birth of a son and that, as a girl, she gained status because she had four brothers. How does this outlook affect Fadumo throughout her life? How does your society value girls and boys?

2. Female circumcision is a powerful tradition in Somalia marking a girl's transition to womanhood. What are some other traditions to mark this transition? According to Fadumo, "Tradition is powerful. It's unthinkable to work against tradition. No girl would want to avoid circumcision, for it would mean exclusion (p. 41)." Do you feel this is an accurate assessment of many cultures' traditions? Presently, do you feel the power of tradition has changed or been lost and to what extent? What traditions do you uphold?

3. What was your reaction when you read of Fadumo's cutting?

4. After being circumcised, Fadumo becomes severely ill. How does her illness affect her personality and her psyche? Why does it take so long for her family to realize how ill she is? At what point does she connect her illness with her circumcision? What immediate and gradual effects does this realization have?

5. Fadumo has a large extended family, some of whom take her in as she travels in search of medical help and some of whom have very powerful political ties. Discuss her relationship with each of these family members. How do these relationships affect Fadumo's road to recovery?

6. Fadumo began her life as a nomad and then spent most of her young life moving from place to place in search of medical attention. In what ways did her life as a nomad prepare her for the travels to come? In what ways did it disadvantage her?

7. Fadumo sees several doctors before she finds one understanding enough to know how to treat her. What do you think of the doctors' responses? How do you think they should have handled the situation?

8. Discuss Fadumo's relationship with Walter. How does this relationship influence Fadumo's view of herself?

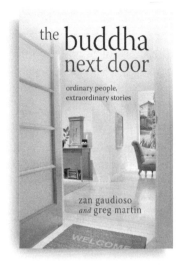

THE BUDDHA NEXT DOOR
Ordinary People, Extraordinary Stories

AUTHORS: *Zan Gaudioso* and *Greg Martin*

PUBLISHER: Middleway Press, July 2007

WEBSITE: www.middlewaypress.com

AVAILABLE IN:
Paperback, 320 pages, $15.95
ISBN: 978-0-9779245-1-6

SUBJECT: Personal Triumph/Inspiration/
Spirituality (Memoir)

"This book is like a warm blanket, my favorite music and a happy heart."
—**Kimberly Kirberger, author of the *Chicken Soup for the Teenage Soul* series.**

SUMMARY: Through dozens of personal experiences, this anthology illuminates how the practice of Nichiren Buddhism has changed people's lives for the better. These first-person narratives—representing folks from all across the country of various ages and ethnic backgrounds—examine the challenges of daily life associated with health, relationships, career, and aging, and the ensuing experiences of hope, success, inspiration, and personal enlightenment that come about as a result of living as Nichiren Buddhists.

ABOUT THE AUTHORS: **Zan Gaudioso** is the contributing author and editor of several volumes of the best-selling *Chicken Soup for the Soul* series including *Chicken Soup for the Teenage Soul III*. She lives in Pacific Palisades, California. **Greg Martin** is co-author of the best-selling book, *The Buddha in Your Mirror*, and a vice general director of the SGI-USA, the lay organization of Nichiren Buddhists in the United States. He lives in Los Angeles.

1. Did you find that the preface and glossary in this book were helpful in understanding the Buddhist rites practiced by the people portrayed in these stories? Did the book inspire you to seek more information about Nichiren Buddhism?

2. Each of the stories tells of an individual faced with personal problems which are overcome by the practice of the Buddhist faith. Which one of these stories resonated most with you and why?

3. Would you like to discover how the lives of the people in these stories have evolved since the publication of the book? What do you think the future holds for them?

4. Soka Gakkai International President Ikeda states that the mission of everyone in their life is "to climb the mountain in front of you." How do the people in this book set out to do this? How far are they successful? Does this describe how you feel about your mission in life?

5. This book is entitled *The Buddha Next Door*. Were you surprised at how many people from different places and from different walks of life are practicing the Buddhist way of life? What does this say about people's search for meaning?

6. The book is divided into seven different chapters, each containing stories pertaining to a certain aspect of human life. Which of these seven appealed most to you and why?

7. The practicing Buddhists portrayed find the answers to their individual challenges within themselves. Daisaku Ikeda is quoted as saying "Who answers our prayers? We do through faith and effort. No one does it for us." Discuss if and how this thought differs from other religious beliefs.

8. Many of the stories tell of overcoming great challenges by using actions inspired by the strength and wisdom developed through chanting. Can you describe any triumphs over adversity gained through similar positive powers of thought, meditation and prayer in your life or the lives of people you know?

9. The Buddhist practice aims to bring people into harmony with the universe so that the individual can attain wisdom, courage, life force and compassion. Do these "ordinary people" manifest these attributes, and are they successful in creating peace in their world? In your opinion, how can these attributes contribute on a larger scale to create peace and harmony in the world at large.

BURNING BRIGHT

AUTHOR: *Tracy Chevalier*

PUBLISHER: Plume, February 2008

WEBSITE: www.penguin.com
www.tchevalier.com

AVAILABLE IN:
Paperback, 320 pages, $14.00
ISBN: (13) 978-0-452-28907-9
ISBN: (10) 0-452-28907-6

SUBJECT: Coming of Age/
Relationships/Social Issues
(Historical Fiction)

*A novel teeming with the complexities of life . . . Chevalier has a fine eye for detail and delightfully captures the sights, smells, and sounds of an earlier time." —**Chicago Sun Times***

"*Chevalier's vivid descriptions and unusual mix of characters make this story an easy pleasure to read." —**Library Journal***

SUMMARY: *Burning Bright* follows the Kellaway family as they leave behind tragedy in rural Dorset and come to late 18th-century London. As they move in next door to the radical painter/poet William Blake, and take up work for a near-by circus impresario, the youngest family member gets to know a girl his age.

Set against the backdrop of a city nervous of the revolution gone sour across the Channel in France, *Burning Bright* explores the states of innocence and experience just as Blake takes on similar themes in his best-known poems, *Songs of Innocence* and *Songs of Experience*.

ABOUT THE AUTHOR: **Tracy Chevalier** is the *The New York Times* bestselling author of four previous novels, including *Girl With a Pearl Earring*, which was translated into thirty-nine languages and made into an Oscar-nominated film. Born and raised in Washington, D.C., she lives in London with her husband and son.

1. Discuss your first impressions of the main characters. Whom did you like best initially? Which, if any, surprised you by the end? Whose transformation was most complete?

2. The Kellaway and Butterfield families, though very different, also have some similarities. Compare and contrast the parental relationships, as well as the sibling relationships, within the two families.

3. Throughout the novel, attention is paid to the differences between city and country, with Maggie and Jem each representing their home turf. Which does Chevalier portray more sympathetically—city (Maggie) or country (Jem)? In what ways?

4. Why do you think Chevalier chose to set her novel in 1792? Why not a few years earlier, or later?

5. William Blake's first two appearances in the novel are quite striking—first, in his *bonnet rouge*, and then when Jem and Maggie spy on him having sex in his backyard. What significance does this have for him as a character? What did you expect of him after these prominent glimpses?

6. Before reading *Burning Bright*, were you familiar with Blake's work? How did it color your experience of the novel?

7. Read and discuss the poem from which the book's title is taken, "The Tyger." What is its significance in terms of the novel and the characters? Why do you think Chevalier chose a phrase from this poem for her title?

8. Two of Blake's most famous works are *Songs of Innocence* and *Songs of Experience*. How do those works relate to the characters of Jem and Maggie?

9. What role does economics—and class—play?

10. *Burning Bright* is set in and around Astley's Circus, a popular real-life attraction in 1790s London. How does Tracy Chevalier use the circus as a character? What does it represent?

11. Laura Devine tells Maisie, "What you want is not worth half the value of what you've still got." What did she mean by that? How might it resonate with Maisie later in the novel? And for the other principal characters?

12. Maggie tries exceptionally hard to preserve Maisie's virginity, eventually turning to William Blake for help. Why does she go this far when nobody else seems to care?

13. How much did you know about the political background of the story? Would you have signed the loyalty oath like the one in the book? What did it reveal about Dick Butterfield's character when he signed? About Thomas Kellaway's when he refused?

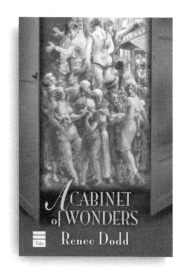

A CABINET OF WONDERS

AUTHOR: **Renee Dodd**

PUBLISHER: Toby Press, September 2006

WEBSITE: www.tobypress.com

AVAILABLE IN:
Hardcover, 320 pages, $24.95
ISBN: 1-59264-164-4

SUBJECT: Social Issues/Relationships/
Personal Challenges (Fiction)

"Dodd makes this strange world come alive. A capable performer in her own right, she juggles multiple plot lines. It's impossible not to be charmed by this vividly drawn crew—their tough exteriors belie tender hearts. . . . A rare treat: a diverting and insightful piece of quirky fiction."
—*Kirkus* (**starred review**)

"Renee Dodd has achieved something wondrous . . . she has taken characters we tend to shun as "other" and made them into ourselves by involving us in their passion, their pain, and their vulnerable, hopeful laughter. A great debut!" —**Chitra Banerjee Divakaruni, author of** *Arranged Marriage: Stories* **and** *Mistress of Spices*

SUMMARY: When the curtains are drawn back on the cabinet of wonders, every individual you meet is an original, the indelible mark of their uniqueness shaped in their flesh. Molly and Faye are spirited teenagers—and conjoined twins. Saffron is the Wolf Girl, her female form covered head to toe in fur. Alex/Alexandra is a seductive morphodite, her male/female parts irresistible to many.

Set in 1927, this marvelous tale confronts the spectacle of the Freak Show, steps through the curtains and out the other side, taking the reader to a candid, complex and human space where they can know outsiders as intimates.

ABOUT THE AUTHOR: **Renee Dodd**, whose name is pronounced "Renny," received an M.F.A. from the University of Houston, and teaches creative writing at Georgia College and State University. She is currently at work on a second novel.

1. The novel begins with a prologue, "Welcome Rubes," which uses the second person to place the reader back in 1927 as a spectator at Dugan's Cabinet of Wonders. Why do you think Dodd chose to start the novel this way?

2. The first chapter, "A Boil Up," is a very intimate, behind the scenes look at some of the everyday concerns of carnival performers. What effect does this chapter have on the reader? What is the combined effect of following the prologue with this scene?

3. What is your opinion regarding Shadrach's belief that Wonders like those in Dugan's show are evidence of the hand of God? How does that opinion apply to contemporary society, where medical advances have drastically reduced these sorts of human variations?

4. Many different kinds of love are discussed in this novel—romantic love, unrequited love, platonic love, family love and so on. How are these kinds of love depicted? In the end, what sort of love seems to be the most valuable?

5. Do you think that working in a freak show exploits the characters in this novel or empowers them? Do you think the same sort of experience would be possible if this show existed in today's world?

6. Take a look at the use of feminine and masculine pronouns used to refer to Alex, both in dialogue and in the narration. Why do some characters seem to think of Alex as female, some as male, and some as both? Why might Dugan mainly see Alex as female, and yet sometimes see her/him as both female and male?

7. Sean requests that Dugan and Mario help him end his life. Why do Dugan and Mario agree to help, and how does doing so affect them? Would you consider Sean's death an act of suicide? Why or why not?

8. What was your reaction to the various stages of development in the twins' sexual awakening? How do Molly and Faye's views of love and romance evolve throughout the novel?

9. Dugan is the patriarchal hub of the novel, and despite his many flaws, he makes for a likeable main character. Why is that? What do you see as Dugan's greatest weakness? His greatest strength? What changes does he go through in the novel? Do you think he is a different man by the time he shows up at Alex's trailer park in Florida?

10. How do you think the big storm in Part Two changed the characters and altered the course of events? Do you think it was the storm that broke the family apart, or do you think it only sped up the inevitable?

CASPIAN RAIN

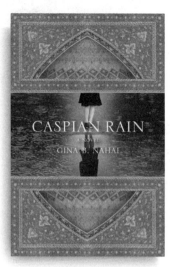

AUTHOR: *Gina B. Nahai*

PUBLISHER: MacAdam/Cage,
            September 2007

WEBSITE: www.macadamcage.com
         www.ginabnahai.com

AVAILABLE IN:
Hardcover, 300 pages, $25.00
ISBN: (13) 978-1-59692-251-8
ISBN: (10) 1-59692-251-6

SUBJECT: Coming of Age/Personal
Challenges/ Cultural & World Issues (Fiction)

" . . . *both a riveting family drama and compelling historical fiction . . . The multiple ways Jews and Muslims intersect is also clearly presented, offering a fascinating glimpse into Persian life prior to the 1979 insurgency. Richly detailed, emotionally intense, and tremendously moving, this work is highly recommended.*" —**Library Journal**

"*In her stirring fourth novel, Nahai explores the struggles of an Iranian family in the tenuous decade before the Islamic revolution . . . a poignant tale of a 'damaged family.'* " —**Publishers Weekly**

SUMMARY: From the best-selling author of *Moonlight on the Avenue of Faith*, a stirring, lyrical tale that offers American readers unique insight into the inner workings of Iranian society.

At once a cultural exploration of an as-yet-unfamiliar society and a psychological study of the effects of loss, *Caspian Rain* takes the reader inside the tragic and fascinating world of a brave young girl struggling against impossible odds.

ABOUT THE AUTHOR: **Gina B. Nahai** is the author of *Cry of the Peacock* (winner of the Los Angeles Arts Council Award for Fiction), *Moonlight on the Avenue of Faith* (finalist for the Orange Prize in England and the IMPAC award in Dublin), and *Sunday's Silence*. Nahai currently lives in Los Angeles.

1. One of the dominant themes in the story is that of loss: Bahar losing her dreams, Yaas losing her hearing and her father, Ruby losing her lover. How does each character respond to his or her great loss? Is that reaction universal, or is it particular to the place and the culture? How would a Westerner react to a similar loss?

2. Bahar marries Omid thinking it will open for her many doors to opportunity. Instead, she becomes the prisoner of limitations. To what extent are these limitations social and cultural, and to what extent do they spring from her personal shortcomings?

3. Given that Omid's controlling Bahar is not very different from the way other men treat their wives at the time, do you think Omid is particularly cruel? Or can his behavior be understood within the social and historical context of the story?

4. Are there choices for Bahar and Yaas that they do not recognize? Could they take a road, in responding to life's hardships, that they aren't able to see because of their own warped perception?

5. With the exception of Ruby and the Tango Dancer, all the women in the story do their best to abide by the rules of their society. This costs them dearly. But Ruby and the Tango Dancer, who do not respect social mores, also pay a great price for their freedom. Which of the two is the wiser way? Do women everywhere have a better chance of finding happiness by living within traditional boundaries, or by challenging them in favor of greater freedom?

6. Chamedooni carries a suitcase full of hope—most of it false or misleading. Does he do his clients a service by giving them that hope? Or is he pushing them into the bottomless hole that the Tango Dancer warns Yaas against?

7. Afterward, Yaas is not certain if her father had indeed promised he would take her along to America, or if she had misunderstood him because of her failing hearing. What do you think happened? Would Omid be capable of such cruelty? Or did Yaas hear what she wanted to hear?

8. Knowing what will become of her parents' meeting, Yaas has a choice in the final chapter: she can prevent the meeting, or let Bahar go on to the future that destroys her. Do you agree with the decision she makes?

9. "What is a life, in the end, but a story we leave behind?" Yaas asks. What does she mean by this?

10. How would you answer Yaas's other question: "What do you do with a loss you can neither cure, nor accept, nor overcome?"

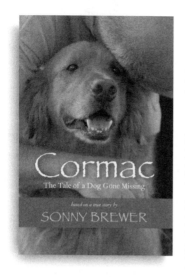

CORMAC
The Tale of a Dog Gone Missing

AUTHOR: *Sonny Brewster*

PUBLISHER: MacAdam/Cage, September 2007

WEBSITE: www.macadamcage.com
www.overthetransom.com

AVAILABLE IN:
Paperback, 200 pages, $13.00
ISBN: (13) 978-1-59692-302-7
ISBN: (10) 1-59692-302-4

ALSO AVAILABLE IN:
Hardcover, 200 pages, $17.00
ISBN: 978-1-59692-061-3

SUBJECT: Memoir/Personal Challenges/
Inspiration (Fiction)

"Everyone who has ever looked down an empty road, waiting for a beloved animal to come walking home, will love this book." —**Rick Bragg, Pulitzer Prize-winning author of** *Ava's Man* **and** *All Over But the Shoutin'*

SUMMARY: In the same vein as *Marley and Me* and *My Dog Skip*, this "mostly true" novel is at once a whimsical campfire mystery and a universal story about the friendship between a man and his dog.

Cormac, a golden retriever who has always been afraid of thunderstorms and lightning flashes, runs away one stormy night while his master is away.

So begins a strange adventure that lands Cormac in the back of a red pickup truck driven by a mysterious woman, takes him to a series of dog pounds and rescue shelters, and ultimately brings him to the suburbs of Connecticut. His owner, meanwhile, devastated by Cormac's disappearance and trying to juggle a family, a book tour, and writing his new novel, becomes determined to solve the "dog-napping" case. With the help of the local veterinarian, bookstore colleagues, animal rescue employees, and old friends, he picks up on Cormac's trail and watches his small-town community come together in search of his lost companion.

Inspired by real events, and embellished only to serve the story through the spirit of imagination, Brewer has, as he says, "mainly told the truth in this story of losing my good dog Cormac."

ABOUT THE AUTHOR: **Sonny Brewer** owns Over the Transom Bookstore in Fairhope, Alabama, and serves as board chairman of the Fairhope Center for the Writing Arts. He is the author of the novel *The Poet of Tolstoy Park* and the upcoming *A Sound like Thunder*.

1. "It's just a dog," someone might say. What is behind the attachment and affection some people feel toward their pets?

2. Do you agree or disagree that dogs have the emotional "feelings" we ascribe to them?

3. What about intelligence? Is a dog's behavioral response more than instinctual?

4. Much is made of the way people feel about their dogs, but what about the old saw that a dog is "man's best friend"? Do they really love us? Are they just looking for the next bowl of food?

5. Dogs love to be petted and stroked. Look into the possibility that there is physiology at play here, a chemical stimulant component for Fido when you ruffle his fur.

6. Rupert Sheldrake, the British biophysicist suggests dogs, and other animals, possess what might be loosely called extrasensory perception. Have you heard of a dog that "knows" when its master is coming home, even though the family does not know Dad's anywhere near?

7. Pierre, in the book, declares he'd say "so long" to the pooch, and, if not "good riddance," at least just trust that the dog is okay wherever the dog happens to be. If your dog "went missing," to what extent would you go to recover her? Do you have a friend who would think extreme efforts to recover a lost pet is time and money not well-spent?

8. How do you feel about mandatory spaying and neutering of all pets, with no exceptions, except when permitted with a special breeder's license?

9. Do you think it's okay to have a dog that's an "outside" dog, like, say, a farm dog that never gets to come inside the house?

10. When an owner names her dog, do you think we mostly "get it right" and find a name that matches the personality of the pooch?

11. Do you think your dog thinks about you when you are not with them, or is it an instant, "Oh, you! I remember you. You feed me and pat my head. I'm glad to see you again!"

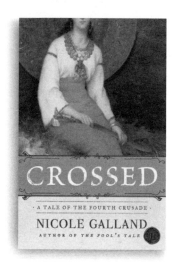

CROSSED
A Tale of the Fourth Crusade

AUTHOR: *Nicole Galland*

PUBLISHER: Harper, February 2008

WEBSITE: www.nicolegalland.com
www.harpercollins.com

AVAILABLE IN:
Hardcover, 656 pages, $15.95
ISBN: 978-0-06-084180-5

SUBJECT: History/Faith/Intrigue (Fiction)

Praise for Nicole Galland's first novel, *The Fool's Tale*:
"Intoxicating, bawdy and thoroughly entertaining . . . Fascinating characters, sophisticated wit, passion, and intrigue make Galland's debut an irresistible read." —Book of the Month Club

SUMMARY: Venice, 1202. Tens of thousands of crusaders set sail for Jerusalem to liberate the great city from Muslim rule. Among them is a British vagabond grudgingly taken under the wing of a pious knight who believes that the mission is truly blessed by God. Before leaving, the vagabond rescues a woman pretending to be an Arab princess, hoping that under the protection of his benefactor knight, he can smuggle the young woman back to the Holy Land. However, this "holy" campaign sinks into tragic moral turpitude—first in an attack on the Adriatic port city of Zara, and ultimately in the dramatic, disastrous sack of the seat of the Byzantine empire, Constantinople.

This book is a rich and riveting tale replete with exotic settings, full-blooded and complex characters, and sparkling wit.

ABOUT THE AUTHOR: Award-winning screenwriter **Nicole Galland** is currently working on her fourth novel, set in Leominster, England. Raised on Martha's Vineyard, she has been an itinerant gypsy for much of her adult life, dividing her time between east and west coasts. However, she has recently married and rumor has it she may settle down soon.

1. Discuss the title of the book. What are all the possible applications of the word *crossed* to the events and characters of the story?

2. Whom do you consider the most sympathetic character in the story? Why?

3. Which character behaves the most honorably throughout? Why?

4. If you were to find yourself in this story, which of the five main characters would you most resemble in outlook and action? (This might be a different response than questions 2 or 3.)

5. Discuss the differences of the two narrators—in their character and background; their morality and values and belief-systems; their storytelling styles.

6. Discuss Dandolo's comments near the end of the book about the fall of empires. Does this seem like a purely historical observation, or are there possible implications about today's world as well?

7. Discuss Jamila's dilemma of having to choose whether she will remain with a man she loves or return to her community. What do you think of the choice she makes, and what choice would you make in her position?

8. What do you think is implied by the end of the epilogue: that the Briton has found a way to join the Jewish community, or that he and Jamila have gone off on their own?

9. There are strong parallels between the Fourth Crusade and the current situation in Iraq, but the author emphasizes these parallels infrequently in the text itself. How often, if ever, did such parallels occur to you as you were reading?

10. Who is a better ruler, Dandolo or Boniface? Why?

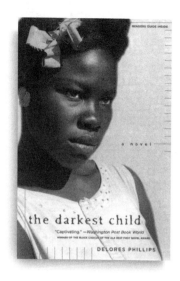

THE DARKEST CHILD

AUTHOR: *Delores Phillips*

PUBLISHER: Soho Press, January 2005

WEBSITE: www.sohopress.com

AVAILABLE IN:
Paperback, 462 pages, $14.00
ISBN: 1-56947-378-1

SUBJECT: Family/Social Issues/
Personal Challenges (Historical Fiction)

"[An] exceptional debut novel. . . . [Has] a depth and dimension not often characteristic of a first novel."—**Library Journal** (**starred review**)

"Phillips writes with a no-nonsense elegance. . . . As a vision of African-American life, The Darkest Child *is one of the harshest novels to arrive in many years. . . . [Phillips] buttresses those harsh episodes with a depth of characterization worthy of Chekhov, pitch-perfect dialogue, and a profound knowledge of the segregated south in the '50s." —**The New Leader**

SUMMARY: Rozelle Quinn is so fair-skinned that she can pass for white. Her ten children are mostly light, too. They constitute the only world she controls and her power over them is all she has in an otherwise cruel and uncaring universe.

Tangy Mae, thirteen, her darkest-complected child, is the brightest. Tangy Mae desperately wants to continue with her education but her mother wants her to work cleaning houses for whites, like she does, and accompany her to the "Farmhouse," where Rozelle earns extra money bedding men.

This is the story from an era when life's possibilities for an African-American were unimaginably different.

ABOUT THE AUTHOR: **Delores Phillips** was born in Bartow County, Georgia. She graduated from Cleveland State University with a Bachelor of Arts in English and works as a nurse at a state psychiatric hospital. Her work has appeared in *Jean's Journal, Black Times,* and *The Crisis.* She lives in Cleveland, Ohio.

1. Rozelle Quinn was the child of a rape which left her mother permanently injured. What effect did this have on Rozelle's upbringing? On her ability to mother her own children? Did she exhibit any maternal feelings toward her children? What instances of good treatment by her mother did Tangy Mae recall?

2. As the book opens, did Tangy Mae really believe her mother was dying? If she did, how could she have remained so innocent? Would things have been different today? How is the loss of Tangy's innocence reflected in her telling of the story? Do you think Rozelle would have explained about "the birds and the bees" to any of her children?

3. Rozelle has been brutal, but she has never killed one of her children until she throws Judy from the porch (Chapter 27). She is convincing when she tells the sheriff it was an accident. Why does Tangy momentarily refuse to believe her own senses? When she thinks "No mother could do that, not even mine. Could she?," who or what is she questioning?

4. Rozelle began to have children long before birth control pills were legal. Do you think she would have used "the pill" if it had been available? Do you think Rozelle hated Judy because she was dark-skinned or because her birth ended Rozelle's childbearing days?

5. What effect did Rozelle's appearance have on her mental condition? What benefit if any did she derive from her beauty? What was the effect upon her of the difference between her treatment by white society and the treatment she would have been accorded if she had been "passing" as white? Did this disparity between appearance and reality have an effect on her mental stability?

6. Why didn't Tarabelle retrieve "the box" while her mother was in the hospital? Why did she wait for her eighteenth birthday? Why is she so much more angry than the other children? Was she justified? Should she have honored her mother even though her mother did not honor her? What were Rozelle's feelings for Tarabelle?

7. Despite everything, Tangy Mae retains her pride and ambition. How has she been able to survive and become a good person? Where does her strength come from? When she leaves at the end of the book, could she have done anything else? Was she selfish to leave? Should she have taken Laura with her?

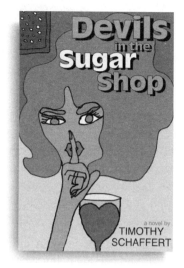

DEVILS IN THE SUGAR SHOP

AUTHOR: *Timothy Schaffert*

PUBLISHER: Unbridled Books, May 2007

WEBSITE: www.unbridledbooks.com

AVAILABLE IN:
Paperback, 256 pages, $14.95
ISBN: (13) 978-1-932961-33-1
ISBN: (10) 1-932961-33-X

SUBJECT: Family/Relationships/ Women's Lives (Fiction)

"Like an expensive box of chocolates: each silken morsel is luscious and approvingly decadent, and with every bite you don't necessarily know what you're going to get." —Library Journal **(starred review)**

"[C]an a novel still be called chick lit if (a) it's written by a guy and (b) most of the chicks in question are in their late 30s to early 40s and not especially interested in shoes? When the characters spend as much time as these do searching for love, sipping cocktails and seeking comfort in one another's company, the answer is yes." —The New York Times Book Review

SUMMARY: *Devils in the Sugar Shop* is the story of a group of women friends in Omaha who are struggling with various romantic troubles and who are all about to convene for a pre-Valentine's Tupperware-like home party for "marital aids." The evening, meant to be a lark, changes how they each view their lives and relationships—and not just their romances but also their friendships and relationships with their children. With his characteristic touch, Schaffert places an unusual cast in unusual circumstances and creates a comic tale that is similar to *Tales of the City*, or even a cross between "Sex and the City" and "Desperate Housewives"—and yet vintage Schaffert.

ABOUT THE AUTHOR: **Timothy Schaffert** is the award-winning author of two previous novels: *The Phantom Limbs of the Rollow Sisters* and *The Singing and Dancing Daughters of God*. He lives in Nebraska, where he is the director of the (Downtown) Omaha Lit Fest and a contributing editor for the *Prairie Schooner* literary journal.

1. Is there an overall message in *Devils in the Sugar Shop*? If so, what is it?

2. Are some parts of the book funny and zany? Which passages are amusing?

3. Which parts are both humorous and sad? Why?

4. What needs are driving the affair between Peach and Troy?

5. Who bears the primary fault for the adulterous relationship? Is it Zeke's responsibility because he has broken his marital vows to Ashley and thus only he is accountable to her? Or is Peach a "home wrecker"?

6. What is going on emotionally between Viv and Zeke? What is motivating their kissing sessions?

7. What could be some of the possible causes for Mrs. Bloom's mental breakdown? In a way, does Viv save Mrs. Bloom's life? What would have happened had Viv not intervened?

8. Why is there a rivalry between Peach and Plum? Do they seem closer by the end of the novel? Why or why not?

9. Is Ashley homophobic? What evidence is there for or against that possibility?

10. What sentiments feed the relationship between Viv, Ashley, and Deedee?

11. Do you agree or disagree with Deedee's idea that ". . . it was impossible to be hip in a youth culture so booby trapped."

12. What do the drag queens symbolize? What is their role in the story?

13. How would you characterize or define Schaffert's overall style of writing?

14. In which passages does he use clever titles or names, real and invented, that seem add to the book's wittiness?

15. What is resolved in the end? What isn't?

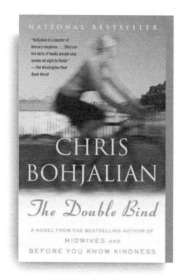

THE DOUBLE BIND

AUTHOR: *Chris Bohjalian*

PUBLISHER: Vintage Books, February 2008

WEBSITE: ww.ReadingGroupCenter.com
www.chrisbohjalian.com

AVAILABLE IN:
Paperback, 448 pages, $14.95
ISBN: 978-1-4000-3166-5

SUBJECT: Social Issues/Intrigue/
Personal Challenges (Fiction)

*"Bohjalian is a master of literary suspense. . . . His are the sorts of books people stay awake all night to finish." —**The Washington Post Book World***

*"Artfully crafted, terrifying. . . . Laurel is an unforgettable, vulnerable, complicated character." —**Los Angeles Times***

SUMMARY: When college sophomore Laurel Estabrook is attacked while riding her bicycle through Vermont's back roads, her life is forever changed. Formerly outgoing, Laurel withdraws into her photography and begins to work at a homeless shelter. It is there she meets Bobbie Crocker, a man with a history of mental illness and a box of photographs that he won't let anyone see. But when Bobbie suddenly dies, Laurel discovers that he was a successful photographer. As Laurel's fascination with Bobbie's former life grows, she becomes convinced that his photographs reveal a deeply hidden secret.

The paperback edition also includes the photographs which were Chris Bohjalian's inspiration in writing *The Double Bind*.

ABOUT THE AUTHOR: **Chris Bohjalian** is the critically acclaimed author of ten novels. He won the New England Book Award in 2002. His novel *Midwives* was a number one *The New York Times* bestseller and an Oprah's Book Club selection. His work has been translated into eighteen languages and published in twenty-one countries, and has twice been adapted into acclaimed movies ("Midwives" and "Past the Bleachers"). Chris graduated from Amherst College, and lives in Vermont with his wife and daughter.

1. Chris Bohjalian begins the novel with a very matter-of-fact description of a brutal attack. Later in the novel, he writes about Laurel, "she preferred black and white [photography] because she thought it offered both greater clarity and deeper insight into her subjects. In her opinion, you understood a person better in black and white." Compare Laurel's analysis of photography to the writing style of the author, particularly in the prologue.

2. Discuss Bohjalian's treatment of homelessness, both as a reality and as an abstraction or social issue.

3. We learn from Laurel that the phrase "Double Bind" is a psychiatric term for a "particular brand of bad parenting [that] could inadvertently spawn schizophrenia." What else, in light of Laurel's mental state, might the title of the book refer to?

4. Is Laurel's imagined life for Bobbie—and all his psychiatric problems—a way for her to express her own psychotic break? Is the Bobbie Crocker that the reader gets to know really a facet of Laurel's personality?

5. Through most of the book the reader believes, along with Laurel, that she escaped certain rape—and that her ability to hold on to her bike saved her. But after the attack, she gives up biking. Discuss the play between the conscious and subconscious mind—a delicate balance that must have underlined all of Laurel's actions—in this abandonment of the very thing she'd convinced herself was her savior.

6. In a feat of narrative turnaround, *The Double Bind* ends with a shocking revelation. Did you find yourself reviewing the novel or rereading it to experience it anew? Did you find the treatment of F. Scott Fitzgerald's characters to be more or less significant in light of the revelation about Laurel's sanity?

7. How was Laurel able to block out what really happened to her when she carried real physical scars of the mutilation to remind her of it? Were there clues in the narrative that part of her did know what happened all along?

*A complete Reading Group Guide can be found inside the book,
or visit www.ReadingGroupCenter.com.*

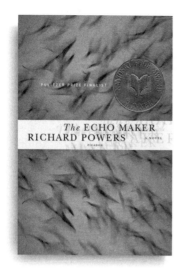

THE ECHO MAKER

AUTHOR: *Richard Powers*

PUBLISHER: Picador USA, August 2007

WEBSITE: www.picadorusa.com

AVAILABLE IN:
Paperback, 464 pages, $15.00
ISBN: (13) 978-0-312-42643-9
ISBN: (10) 0-312-42643-7

SUBJECT: Family/Intrigue/Identity
(Fiction)

Winner of the 2006 National Book Award

"In The Echo Maker, *Powers hopes to plumb the nature of consciousness, and he does so with such alert passion that we come to recognize in his quest the novel's abiding theme. . . . What it means to be human will forever elude us."* —**Los Angeles Times Book Review**

"A grand novel—grand in its reach, grand in its themes, grand in it patterning. . . . If Powers were an American writer of the nineteenth century . . . he'd probably be the Herman Melville of Moby-Dick. *His picture is that big."* —**Margaret Atwood, The New York Review of Books**

SUMMARY: On a remote Nebraska road, twenty-seven-year-old Mark Schluter has a near-fatal car accident. His older sister, Karin, returns reluctantly to their hometown to nurse Mark back from a traumatic head injury. But when Mark emerges from a coma, he believes that this woman is really an imposter. When Karin contacts the famous cognitive neurologist Gerald Weber for help, he diagnoses Mark as having Capgras Syndrome.

The mysterious nature of the disease, combined with the strange circumstances surrounding Mark's accident, threatens to change all of their lives beyond recognition.

ABOUT THE AUTHOR: **Richard Powers** is the author of nine novels. *The Echo Maker* was a finalist for the Pulitzer Prize. Powers has received a MacArthur Fellowship, a Lannan Literary Award, and the James Fenimore Cooper Prize for Historical Fiction. He lives in Illinois.

1. What echoes do the cranes create throughout the novel? What do the cranes signify to those who admire them—tourists, environmentalists, local residents along the Platte River? What parallels exist between the echo of the migrating birds and the echoes lurking in Mark's shattered memory?

2. How would you characterize the sibling dynamics between Mark and Karin? How much of their former relationship remains intact after his accident? Would you have sacrificed as much as Karin did to help an injured brother or sister?

3. How does Bonnie cope with Dr. Weber's assertion that faith in God has a neurological component?

4. Discuss the Nebraska landscape as if it were a character in the novel. What makes it alluring as well as daunting? In what way does the region's "personality" mirror that of its inhabitants?

5. Is Mark or Karen on a path, perhaps even unwittingly, of carrying on their parents' legacies?

6. What contemporary environmental concerns are reflected in the showdown over the Central Platte Scenic Natural Outpost?

7. Were you suspicious of Barbara in the novel's early chapters? How did your perception of her shift? How would you have responded if you had been in her position on the night of the accident?

8. In part three, Karin tells Daniel she thinks Mark might have been better off if she had stayed away. How can we know the difference between selfless and self-serving caregiving?

9. What aspects of body, soul, and memory are presented in the epigraphs appearing throughout the book? Taken by themselves, do these quotations underscore or contradict one another?

10. In what ways did Gerald take on a fatherly role for Karin and Mark? Was their perception of him any more accurate than that of the fans who attended his lectures or saw him on television?

11. Did Capgras syndrome make any aspects of Mark's perception crystal clear or even closer to reality than his caregivers' view of life? What universal experiences are reflected in his inability to accept the identity of someone who loves him, or, near the end, to acknowledge that he is fully alive?

12. What does Karin have to discover about the mind's ability to shape memories? How does her understanding of her past change throughout Mark's illness?

13. What is unique about Power's approach to topics as far-ranging as science and history, deception, and devotion?

EYE CONTACT

AUTHOR: *Cammie McGovern*

PUBLISHER: Penguin Books, April 2007

WEBSITE: www.cammiemcgovern.com

AVAILABLE IN:
Paperback, 320 pages, $ 14.00
ISBN 978-0-143-03890-0

SUBJECTS: Family, Intrigue (Fiction)

"Eye Contact is a page-turner, and I tore through it in twenty-four hours. But it's more than that—it's also a nuanced, poignant exploration of how all of us, with or without autism, struggle to find our place in the world. Cammie McGovern writes with grace and compassion."
—**Curtis Sittenfeld, author of *Prep***

SUMMARY: As children wage mock battles in the playground of Woodside Elementary School, two students, a little girl and boy, seem to vanish, last seen heading toward the woods behind the school. Hours pass and then only one of them, Adam, a nine-year-old boy with autism, is found alive, the sole witness to the girl's murder. Barely verbal on the best of days, Adam has retreated into a silent world that Cara, his mother, knows only too well. With her community in shock and her son unable to help with the police investigation, Cara tries to decode the puzzling events.

ABOUT THE AUTHOR: **Cammie McGovern** was awarded a creative writing fellowship at Stanford University and has received numerous prizes for her short fiction. Her stories have appeared in several magazines and journals, and she is the author of another novel, *The Art of Seeing*. She lives in Amherst, Massachusetts, with her husband and three children, the eldest of whom is autistic. She is one of the founders of Whole Children, a resource center that runs after-school classes and programs for children with special needs.

1. Cara is not the only parent in the book who struggles with raising a child with special needs. Morgan's mother, Kevin's mother, and Amelia's mother are all in similar situations. What are the differences between the ways that they treat their children? Do you think that some of the mothers fail where others have succeeded? What do you agree and disagree with in each of their situations?

2. How different would the search for Amelia's murderer have been if Adam had been an average nine-year-old? What kind of obstacles would have been avoided? What new difficulties would the police have faced?

3. In the aftermath of a tragedy, people surrounding the victims often have feelings of regret, wishing they had done something differently that might have prevented what happened. Have you ever been through a situation like this one? How did you cope with your feelings of guilt and regret? How does June cope with hers?

4. Many of Cara and Suzette's misunderstandings revolve around Kevin and the feelings each of them has for him. What reasons do you think that each of them has for caring about Kevin? Do you think their friendship might have lasted if they had confronted Kevin when they were younger?

5. What does the title "Eye Contact" mean to you?

6. What do you think about Morgan's mother's comment—is it "fine" not to have any friends?

7. Discuss some of the terrible things children do to one another in *Eye Contact* and whether you've observed this kind of behavior in young children you know. What are some of the ways this kind of cruelty can be prevented?

8. One of the results of Adam's autism is his appreciation for classical music and his love of opera. Why do you think that a child who has such a difficult time with language and communication loves music so much? What are his musical talents compensating for? How might they be able to enrich his future life?

9. Morgan is convinced that if he finds out who killed Amelia, he will be forgiven for the crime he committed. Many of the characters in *Eye Contact* are in search of a similar kind of redemption. Do you think any of them are capable of achieving it? In light of this theme of redemption, how do you feel about where the different characters end up at the book's conclusion?

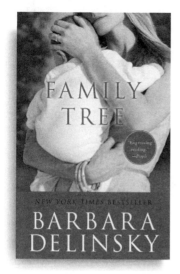

FAMILY TREE

AUTHOR: **Barbara Delinsky**

PUBLISHER: Broadway Books,
October 2007

WEBSITE: www.barbaradelinsky.com
www.broadwaybooks.com

AVAILABLE IN:
Paperback, 384 pages, $14.00
ISBN: 978-0-7679-2518-1

SUBJECT: Family/Social Issues (Fiction)

"Full of complex and fascinating family dynamics as its characters are forced to come to terms with issues such as faith, race, and loyalty, Family Tree *is thought provoking and memorable. . . . Delinsky will be 'discovered' by a new generation of readers."* —**Bookpage**

"Delinsky smoothly challenges characters and readers alike to confront their hidden hypocrisies." —**Publishers Weekly**

"A page-turner that you'll be discussing with your friends." —**News and Sentinel**

"Fail-safe delivery of an issue-packed story perfect for reading groups." —**Kirkus**

SUMMARY: This is the story of Dana and Hugh Clarke, a wealthy, white East Coast couple whose beautiful newborn child clearly has African ancestors. The infant, Lizzie, raises accusations and doubt among all of her parents' relatives. As they gradually piece together the facts, a shocking truth emerges that will forever change this family–while opening their eyes to the real meaning of identity and unconditional love. *Family Tree* raises provocative questions about how we define family, how we view ancestry, and whether racism still lurks in even the most open minds.

ABOUT THE AUTHOR: **Barbara Delinsky** is the author of more than sixteen *New York Times* bestselling novels. A lifelong New Englander, she and her husband have three sons, two daughters-in-law, and a cat. There are more than twenty million copies of her books in print.

1. How would you have reacted if you had experienced Dana and Hugh's situation? How would your circle of friends and coworkers have reacted?

2. Discuss the parallel stories woven throughout the novel, including Dana's painful reunion with her father, Ellie Jo's secret regarding her husband's other marriage, and Crystal's paternity case against the senator. What are the common threads within these family secrets?

3. Should men always be financially obligated to their children, regardless of the circumstances? If so, what should those financial obligations be?

4. Why is it so difficult for Dana to feel anything but anger toward her father? In your opinion, did he do anything wrong? How does she cope with the shifting image of her mother?

5. What is the root of Hugh's reaction in the novel's initial chapters? Is he a racist? Is he torn between loyalties? Does he trust his wife?

6. Is your own ancestry homogenous? If not, what interesting or ironic histories are present in your ancestry? Do you believe it's important to maintain homogeneity in a family tree? If you were to adopt a child, what would be your main criterion in selecting him or her?

7. Discuss the many differences between Dana's and Hugh's families. What drew Dana and Hugh to each other? To what extent is financial power a factor in shaping their attitudes toward the world? What common ground existed despite their tremendous differences in background?

8. What accounts for the universal fascination with genealogy? Should a person be lauded for the accomplishments of an ancestor, or snubbed for the misdeeds of one? Is genealogy a predictor?

9. If you were to undergo DNA mapping, what revelations would please you? What revelations would disappoint you?

10. What role does location play in *Family Tree*? Would the story have unfolded differently within the aristocracy of the South, or in a West Coast city?

11. Who in your life would stand by you after a revelation like Corinne's?

12. Is your neighborhood racially integrated? How many people of color hold executive positions at the top companies in your community? Is there a gulf between the ideal and the reality of a color-blind society in 21st–century America?

THE FEMALE BRAIN

AUTHOR: *Louann Brizendine, M.D.*

PUBLISHER: Broadway Books,
August 2007

WEBSITE: www.broadwaybooks.com
www.thefemalebrain.com

AVAILABLE IN:
Paperback, 304 pages, $14.95
ISBN: 978-0-7679-2010-0

SUBJECT: Women's Lives/Self Help
(Nonfiction)

"*The Female Brain is sassy, witty, reassuring, and great fun. All women—and the men who love them—should read this book.*"
—**Christiane Northrup, M.D., author of** *The Wisdom of Menopause*

"*In a breezy, playful style, Brizendine follows the development of women's brains from birth through the teen years, to courting, pregnancy, childbirth and child-rearing, and on to menopause and beyond.*"
—**Deborah Tannen,** *Washington Post*

SUMMARY: Nature or nurture? Which can best explain the differences between male and female interactions—from the intensity of female friendships to the laws of sexual attraction? Pioneering neuropsychiatrist, Louann Brizendine, M.D delivers the latest findings about the physiology behind a woman's mind. Explaining both the structure of the female brain as well as the intricate hormonal dance that unfolds throughout a lifetime, Dr. Brizendine distills essential truths and dismisses harmful myths. Brimming with eye-opening facts, *The Female Brain* presents a remarkable tour of the innate distinctions between male and female impulses.

ABOUT THE AUTHOR: **Louann Brizendine**, M.D., is a neuropsychiatrist at the University of California, San Francisco, and the founder of the Women's and Teen Girls' Mood and Hormone Clinic. She is a graduate of the Yale University School of Medicine and the University of California, Berkeley, in neurobiology. She lives in the San Francisco Bay area with her husband and son.

1. How did years of emphasis on male subjects skew medical treatment for women and men alike? What did it take for physicians such as Dr. Brizendine to turn the tide?

2. Discuss the book's discussion of gender and aggression in young children. Should our expectations of "acceptable" childhood behavior be altered in recognition of these innate patterns?

3. How does an understanding of the adolescent female brain ease or even alleviate your own memories of teenage angst? Considering the way pleasure centers are stoked by gossip and sexual attractiveness takes priority, is it futile to try to tame the teen-girl brain?

4. What is the best way to reconcile the fact that most girls shun conflict while boys often enjoy it? What are the benefits and challenges of this contradiction? How do the adult manifestations of these features play out in the workplace?

5. Which aspects of Melissa and Rob's case study regarding dating resonated the most with you?

6. What surprised you in Dr. Brizendine's chapter on sexual satisfaction? Did her distinctions between male and female orgasms differ from what you had previously believed? Does twenty-first-century dating accommodate these inherent gender differences?

7. What are the implications of the "mommy brain" for working mothers of newborns? Would it be beneficial or destructive if more fathers experienced the "daddy brain," even extreme manifestations such as Couvade Syndrome? Do women inherently want to share the tasks of parenting?

8. With a better understanding of the inherently different communication styles possessed by men and women, can relationship woes be eased? Or is the communication gulf cause for despair?

9. Does American society embrace the wisdom of menopausal and postmenopausal women? Do contemporary grandmothers receive greater or less respect than in previous generations?

10. What predictions can you make about shifting perceptions of gender wars in a culture that becomes more aware of neuroscience?

11. How might the types of data revealed in Appendix Three shape future discussions about sexual orientation?

12. What research question would you want to explore if you were to design a study regarding the female brain?

13. In what ways does the "Phases of a Female's Life" chart help explain your past behavior and predict your future responses?

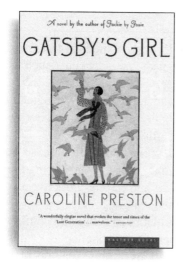

GATSBY'S GIRL

AUTHOR: *Caroline Preston*

PUBLISHER: Mariner Books, May 2007

WEBSITE: www.marinerbooks.com

AVAILABLE IN:
Paperback, 336 pages, $13.95
ISBN: (13) 978-0-618-87261-9
ISBN: (10) 0-618-87261-2

SUBJECT: History/Relationships/
Personal Discovery (Fiction)

A Book Sense Notable

"Preston employs immaculate research and a rich imagination. . . . A fascinating rendering of the tragedy that was Fitzgerald's life and of the young woman who was the catalyst for so much of his glorious body of work." —**Library Journal** (starred review)

"Should be read by anyone interested in Fitzgerald's work [or] the times in which he lived." —**Book Page**

"A wonderfully elegiac novel that evokes the tenor and times of the 'Lost Generation'. . . marvelous." —**Denver Post**

SUMMARY: Before he wrote some of the twentieth century's greatest fiction, before he married Zelda, F. Scott Fitzgerald loved Ginevra, a fickle young Chicago socialite he met during the winter break from Princeton. Ginevra would be the model for many of Fitzgerald's coolly fascinating but unattainable heroines.

In this captivating and moving novel, Caroline Preston imagines what life might have been like for Fitzgerald's first love, following Ginevra from her gilded youth as the daughter of a tycoon through disillusioned marriage and motherhood. An engrossing fictional portrait, *Gatsby's Girl* deftly explores the relationship between a famous author and his muse.

ABOUT THE AUTHOR: **Caroline Preston** is the author of two previous novels, *Jackie by Josie*, a *New York Times* Notable Book of the Year, and *Lucy Crocker 2.0*. A graduate of Dartmouth College, she earned her master's degree in American civilization at Brown University.

1. For the epigraph of *Gatsby's Girl*, Caroline Preston offers a line from F. Scott Fitzgerald's classic novel *The Great Gatsby*: "He talked a lot about the past and I gathered that he wanted to recover something, some idea of himself perhaps, that had gone into loving Daisy . . ." How does Fitzgerald's comment on Jay Gatsby and Daisy Buchanan also bring to mind Preston's account of the relationship between Fitzgerald and Ginevra Perry? How might Fitzgerald's fiction writing have been a way for him to recover something of his own past?

2. Why do you suppose Preston chose fiction as a way to examine the romance between Ginevra and Scott? What artistic freedom does fiction offer that nonfiction does not? How might this have been a different book had it been history rather than historical fiction?

3. What privileges do Gillian's father's status and money afford her? Alternatively, what privations are inherent in her upbringing? How are both Ginevra and Scott shaped by their perceptions of social class?

4. The interplay between fact and fiction figures prominently in Preston's novel; the novel itself offers fictional re-creations of actual events. How does Preston balance reality and imagination in the novel?

5. What comment does the novel make on the legacy of the Jazz Age? How does the book work as a commentary on the literary legacy of F. Scott Fitzgerald?

6. Consider Ginevra's relationships with Scott, Billy, Julian, and John. Is any single relationship wholly fulfilling? What does each offer her? Which man do you suppose sees her most clearly, understands her best, and why?

7. When Ginevra and Scott finally meet again at the Beverly Wilshire in Los Angeles, Scott says to her, "I've faithfully avoided seeing you all these years . . . I wanted to keep my illusion of you perfect." Do you think Ginevra was ultimately worthy of his prolonged interest and attention? Why has Scott so carefully preserved his memory of her?

8. Why do you think that Ginevra hid Scott's letters and refused to talk about their romance? What regrets do you think Ginevra felt at the end of her life?

9. If you have read F. Scott Fitzgerald's own work, what similarities and differences are there between Ginevra Perry and Daisy Buchanan in *The Great Gatsby* or Josephine Perry in Fitzgerald's *The Basil and Josephine Stories*?

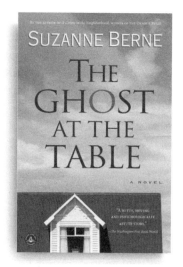

THE GHOST AT THE TABLE

AUTHOR: **Suzanne Berne**

PUBLISHER: Algonquin Books of Chapel Hill, November 2007

WEBSITE: www.algonquin.com

AVAILABLE IN:
Paperback, 304 pages, $13.95
ISBN: 978-1-56512-579-7

SUBJECT: Family/Identity/ Women's Lives (Fiction)

"Evocative. . . . An excellent book club choice." —**Nancy Pearl, NPR commentator and author of** *Book Lust*

"A witty, moving and psychologically astute story about siblings and the disparate ways they remember common experiences from childhood. . . . Wholly engaging, the perfect spark for launching a rich conversation around your own table once the dishes have been cleared." —**The Washington Post Book World**

SUMMARY: Strikingly different since childhood and leading dissimilar lives now, sisters Frances and Cynthia have managed to remain "devoted" —as long as they stay on opposite coasts. When Frances arranges to host Thanksgiving at her New England farmhouse, she envisions a happy family reunion, one that will include the sisters' long-estranged father. Cynthia, however, doesn't understand how Frances can ignore the past their father's presence revives, a past that includes suspicions about their mother's death twenty-five years earlier. As Thanksgiving arrives, with a houseful of guests, the sisters continue to struggle with different versions of a shared past, their conflict escalating to a dramatic, suspenseful climax.

ABOUT THE AUTHOR: **Suzanne Berne** is the author of two novels, *A Crime in the Neighborhood*, which won Great Britain's Orange Prize and was a finalist for both the *Los Angeles Times* and Edgar Allen Poe first fiction Awards, and *A Perfect Arrangement*, a *New York Times* Notable Book.

1. What do you think changed Cynthia's mind in going to Frances's house for Thanksgiving? Why is it so important to Frances to have Cynthia come to her house for the holiday?

2. In addition to Frances's family, other guests come to Frances's house for Thanksgiving. Jane goes so far as to call it "Thanksgiving at the UN" (page 30). What impact do the outsiders have on shaping the events of the evening?

3. At the Thanksgiving table, Frances's daughter Sarah proposes that they take turns describing what they are most proud of having done for someone else (pages 207–11). Compare the answers of each sister. Why does Cynthia find Frances's answer so difficult to hear?

4. *The Ghost at the Table* opens with a quotation from *The Autobiography of Mark Twain*, "a person's memory has no more sense than his conscience." How does this statement pertain to each sister? To what degree does it explain Cynthia's and Frances's different recollections of the past?

5. Both Cynthia and Frances have very different views of their childhood. More specifically, they have opposing accounts of what happened to their mother. Whose version is more credible, and why? Discuss the possibility that both sisters' recollections are accurate.

6. At one point, Cynthia remembers her sister Helen asking their mother what the mother looked like when she was a girl. Instead of listening to her mother's answer, Cynthia is struck "by an appalling, fascinating thought: What if you looked into the future and didn't recognize yourself? What if you saw someone else looking back at you instead?" (page 131–32). Do you think Cynthia the child would recognize Cynthia the adult? Would your childhood self be able to identify the adult you've become?

7. In Cynthia's mind, Frances's daughters, Sarah and Jane, roughly correspond with Frances and herself when they were younger. Is Cynthia simply projecting? In what ways does the past continue to influence the characters' perceptions of the present?

8. Soon after her mother's death, Cynthia implies that her father played a hand in it. She then goes on to tell Frances that Frances unknowingly helped him (pages 155–57). A few days later, though, she retracts the accusation. Do you think she was being honest or dishonest in either case?

9. Who, or what, does the ghost of the title refer to, and why?

GRUB

AUTHOR: *Elise Blackwell*

PUBLISHER: Toby Press, September 2007

WEBSITE: www.tobypress.com

AVAILABLE IN:
Hardcover, 380 pages, $24.95
ISBN: 978-1-59264-199-4

SUBJECT: Identity/Humor/Social Issues (Fiction)

Book Sense Pick

"A fizzy contemporary-Manhattan retelling of New Grub Street. . . . *A quick-paced, amusing novel."* —**Kirkus Reviews**

"In this deliciously mordant send-up of the publishing world, Elise Blackwell conjures up a universe filled with talentless novelists, reptilian publishers, unprincipled agents and brain-dead critics. Thank God this is only a fantasy."—**Joe Queenan, bestselling author and book reviewer for** *The New York Times Book Review*

"Grub is a mordantly witty, thoroughly stimulating absolutely wonderful, satire of the New York literary world and of the price of being a literary success in America." —**The Islamorada Free Press**

SUMMARY: Eddie, on the brink of failure after his critically acclaimed first book, wants only to publish another novel and hang on to his beautiful wife, Amanda, who has her own literary ambitions and a bit of a roving eye. Among their circle are writers of every stripe—from the Machiavellian Jackson to the 'experimental writer' Henry who lives in squalor while seeking the perfect sentence. Amid an assortment of scheming agents, editors, and hangers-on, each writer must negotiate the often competing demands of success and integrity, all while grappling with inner demons and the stabs of professional and personal jealousy. The Devil-Wears-Prada meets Publishing!

ABOUT THE AUTHOR: **Elise Blackwell** is the author of *The Unnatural History of Cypress Parish* and *Hunger*, chosen by the *Los Angeles Times* as one of the best books of 2003. Originally from southern Louisiana, she teaches at the University of South Carolina.

1. Jackson Miller and Eddie Renfros are both friends and rivals. Which one would you argue is the novel's hero? Which one is more sympathetic? Does Jackson possess any endearing traits? What are Eddie's flaws? Does Amanda make the logical choice in choosing one over the other?

2. The title of the novel refers to both *New Grub Street* and the posh restaurant where Doreen works. What connotations does the word "grub" have, and how are they present in the novel?

3. *Grub* can be read as a satire, and its characters as "types." For instance, Henry Baffler is a classic starving artist, while Amanda Renfros can be read as a heartless social climber. Do such characters illuminate human types outside of fiction? Do you think the characters in *Grub* are based on actual people? Does the world of *Grub* mirror contemporary commercial publishing?

4. To what extent are the "unsuccessful" writers, particularly Margot Yarborough and Henry Baffler, responsible for their own fates? To what extent are they victims of the publishing business? Would you say that they are happier or more miserable than the writers who decide to write for a more popular audience?

5. Do any of the "novels" within the novel sound like books you would want to read? Would you rather read *Conduct* or *Sea Miss* by Eddie Renfros? Does Margot's *Pontchartrain* sound like a novel worth reading? What about the novels penned by Jackson and Amanda? Why or why not?

6. Writing in *The Guardian*, D. J. Taylor claims that *New Grub Street* is "one of those terrible books-terrible, that is, to anyone who has ever picked up a pen in earnest-in which every piece of human psychology on display is fatally bound up with the circumstances of literary production." He notes that "the characters who succeed in their ambitions are generally those who care least about literature." Can the same be said of *Grub*? Why do you think the author dedicated the book to "every writer with an unpublished novel?"

7. While living as part of a museum exhibit of writers, Henry Baffler worries that the novel itself has become a "museum piece." Is the literary novel a historical artifact, or is its future brighter than the one Henry sees for it? What makes you think so?

HEAT

An Amateur's Adventures as Kitchen Slave, Line Cook, Pasta-Maker, and Apprentice to a Dante-Quoting Butcher in Tuscany

AUTHOR: *Bill Buford*

PUBLISHER: Vintage Books, June 2007

WEBSITE: www.ReadingGroupCenter.com

AVAILABLE IN:
Paperback, 336 pages, $14.95
ISBN: 978-1-4000-3447-5

SUBJECT: Biography/Humor/Culture (Memoir)

"A superbly detailed picture of life in a top restaurant kitchen . . . Heat *is a sumptuous meal." —The New York Times*

"Delightful. . . . Charming. . . . [Buford's] style is . . . happily obsessed with a weird subculture, woozily in love with both cooking and the foul-mouthed, refined-palette world of the chef." —The Washington Post Book World

SUMMARY: *Heat* started out as an article Buford wrote for *The New Yorker* food issue in 2002 about working in the kitchen of Mario Batali's three-star restaurant, Babbo. The impetus for the article—Buford's desire to learn how professional chefs are different than home cooks—quickly became a full-fledged obsession. From attempting to carry a newly slaughtered pig back from the green market to his Manhattan apartment, to his quest to learn the history of pasta right down to when the egg first appeared, Buford imbues all of his adventures with his trademark energy and hilarity. Amid all of this, Buford offers a behind-the-scenes look at Batali's grandeur and the history of food itself. *Heat*, an enthralling work, examines the very nature of how we eat and what it says about our culture.

ABOUT THE AUTHOR: **Bill Buford** is a staff writer and European correspondent for *The New Yorker*. He was the fiction editor of the magazine for eight years, from April 1995 to December 2002. Before that he edited *Granta* magazine for sixteen years and, in 1989, became the publisher of Granta Books. He has edited three anthologies: *The Best of Granta Travel, The Best of Granta Reportage,* and *The Granta Book of the Family.* Born in Baton Rouge, Louisiana, in 1954, Bill Buford grew up in California. He currently lives in New York City with his wife, Jessica Green, and their two sons.

1. Buford says, "I came to regard the prep kitchen as something like a culinary boot camp." In what ways do the other chefs, Elisa in particular, appear almost militaristic in their approach to cooking? How does Buford's description of the psychical exhaustion he endures help convey the similarities between the Babbo kitchen and boot camp?

2. Mario Batali tells Buford, "You learn by working in the kitchen. Not by reading a book or watching a television program or going to cooking school." While Batali has done this in his own career, he is also the host of several cooking shows and author of several cookbooks. Do you agree that the best way to learn to cook is in the kitchen? What have you learned from cooking shows and cookbooks?

3. When the Babbo cookbook is about to be published, Batali tells his staff that they will have to come up with new recipes since all of the secrets of Babbo will be revealed. Would knowing a restaurant's recipes alter your dining experience? Why or why not?

4. Dario and Batali try to waste as little as possible. Likewise, when Buford brings home the pig from the green market, he uses all of it except for the lungs. Aside from the obvious financial motivations, why are all of these men unwilling to let any food go to waste?

5. Buford is completely flummoxed by the lack of interest among the professionals he encounters in the history of pasta. Why do you think Buford is so obsessed with finding out when the egg first appeared in pasta dough? In what ways does he differ from the professionals that he encounters?

6. Throughout *Heat*, Buford argues that "food is a concentrated messenger of a culture." What are some of the examples he gives to illustrate his point? Can you think of any examples of this in your own life?

7. Dario sees himself not as a businessman or butcher but, rather, as an artisan. How does this impact the way that he runs his shop and interacts with his customers? What does Buford mean when he calls Dario "an artist, whose subject was loss"?

8. Has *Heat* changed your views on dining out and the world of professional cooking? If so, how?

For the complete Reading Group Guide,
visit www.ReadingGroupCenter.com.

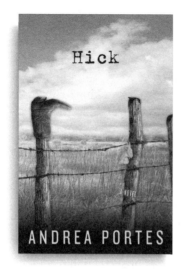

HICK

AUTHOR: *Andrea Portes*

PUBLISHER: Unbridled Books, May 2007

WEBSITE: www.unbridledbooks.com

AVAILABLE IN:
Paperback, 265 pages, $14.95
ISBN: (13) 978-1-932961-32-4
ISBN: (11) 1-932961-32-1

SUBJECTS: Family/Coming of Age/
Identity (Fiction)

"[A] knockout . . . [a] bold, brash, up-yours coming-of-age story rubbed raw with gritty sexual awakening." —**The San Diego Union-Tribune**

SUMMARY: *Hick* is the story of Luli McMullen—feisty, precocious, and out on her own at 13. Luli is running away from Nebraska to Las Vegas, where she plans to escape her disturbing present and even less hopeful future by finding herself a sugar daddy. That Luli finds trouble on the road almost immediately is no surprise. What is a surprise is that regardless of circumstances, Luli refuses to be a victim, even at her tender age. On her perilous journey west, she learns the truth of American rootlessness and discovers both the power and the peril of her own sexual curiosity.

Hick is quite a ride—raw and edgy, hilarious, hopeful and heartbreaking. It's at once a true-to-life portrait of an inviolable spirit threatened by drugs and alcohol, teen sex and crime, and a stubbornly idealistic novel about growing up in America.

ABOUT THE AUTHOR: *Hick* is loosely based on **Andrea Portes'** own childhood. Portes is a young writer who is becoming a cultural force in the hippest parts of Los Angeles. She grew up outside Lincoln, Nebraska, later shuffling between Illinois, Texas, Brazil, North Dakota, and North Carolina before attending Bryn Mawr College. She received her MFA in Theater from UC San Diego and became a script reader for Paramount Pictures. She is a nightlife columnist for several websites.

1. How did you react, overall, to this novel? To the characters? To what happens to Luli?

2. Did you find the events of the novel and Luli's reaction to them believable? If so why? If not, why not? If someone were to say to you that this novel "lives in the voice of Luli," what do you think they might mean by that?

3. Did you find the book funny? If so, how would you describe the humor in it? If not, why not?

4. How would you describe the tone of the novel?

5. What are some of the themes you can identify in the novel? What elements of the novel lead you to identify those themes?

6. How does the setting of the novel interact or contribute to the themes of the novel and the way you read it?

7. How would you describe Luli to someone? Why?

8. Describe the other characters in the novel, including the minor ones, like Luli's school teacher. How, if at all, do they help move the plot and expose the thematic issues in the novel? How do they contribute to the development of other characters in the novel, especially Luli?

9. How realistic or well rounded did you find the characters in the novel? Are there parts of the story that make you feel sympathetic towards Tammy and Nick? If so, what are they? What do they add to the over all richness, or not, of the narrative?

10. How would you describe the author's apparent point of view about why people act the way they do in this world? Do you agree with her, or find it convincing? If so, why? If not, why not?

11. How do you interpret the ending, or the resolution of the novel? What are your feelings about Luli and her future? What led you to your conclusions?

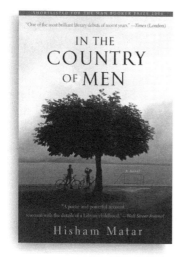

IN THE COUNTRY OF MEN

AUTHOR: *Hisham Matar*

PUBLISHER: Dial Press, March 2008

WEBSITE: www.dialpress.com

AVAILABLE IN:
Paperback, 256 pages, $12.00
ISBN: (13) 978-0-385-34043-4
ISBN: (10) 0-385-34043-5

SUBJECT: Relationships/Cultural &
World Issues/Family (Fiction)

"A poetic and powerful account . . . resonant with the details of a Libyan childhood." —The Wall Street Journal

"Matar writes in a voice that shifts gracefully between the adult exile looking back and the young boy experiencing these events through his limited, confused point of view. . . . This sad, beautiful novel captures the universal tragedy of children caught in their parents' terrors." —**Washington Post Book World**

"At its intimate center, the novel calibrates the boy's shifting, decreasingly innocent perspective as he himself becomes implicated by cruelty and betrayal." —Atlanta Journal-Constitution

SUMMARY: Libya, 1979. Nine-year-old Suleiman's days are circumscribed by the narrow rituals of childhood: outings to the ruins surrounding Tripoli, games with friends played under the burning sun, exotic gifts from his father's constant business trips abroad. But his nights have come to revolve around his mother's increasingly disturbing bedside stories full of old family bitterness. And then one day Suleiman sees his father across the square of a busy marketplace. Wasn't he supposed to be away on business yet again? Why did he lie?

Suleiman is soon caught up in a world he cannot hope to understand—where everything seems mysterious and dangerous.

ABOUT THE AUTHOR: **Hisham Matar** was born in 1970 in New York City to Libyan parents and spent his childhood in Tripoli and Cairo. He lives in London and is currently at work on his second novel.

1. What is the effect of reading about this episode in history through a child's point of view? What clarity does it bring? In what ways do a child's impulses muddy the truth?
2. How would you characterize Muammar al-Qaddafi's political rhetoric as it is captured in the novel?
3. What distinctions exist between experiencing alcoholism in the West and facing it in a locale where religious law forbids drinking?
4. Discuss the title of the novel: *In the Country of Men*. Do the women in Suleiman's life have any true power, and if so, from where is it derived? What does he come to understand about the power hierarchies of Libyan men, and the reasons his father lost his social rank?
5. What had you previously known about Muammar al-Qaddafi and the effects of Italian colonization on Libya? As a supplement to your reading of *In the Country of Men*, discuss articles tracing Qaddafi's unusual story, from being suspected of involvement in the bombing of Pan Am flight 103 over Lockerbie, Scotland, to his recent denunciation of the 9/11 terrorists and the U.S. State Department's May 2006 removal of Libya from a list of countries that sponsor terrorism. Could the novel's characters ever have predicted such an outcome?
6. What is Suleiman's understanding of the events he sees on television, culminating in the execution of Ustath Rashid? When is he able to reconcile the innocent images of noble men with the horrific ones that dominate his mind in the novel's later chapters?
7. What were your impressions of Suleiman's place within his circle of friends? What was it like to see Osama used as an ordinary name for an ordinary little boy? How had Suleiman's feelings toward his friends changed when he was reunited with them years later?
8. What might have become of Suleiman, of his father, of his beloved Siham, if he had never emigrated?
9. Discuss the notion of living as an expatriate. How did Suleiman cope with the knowledge that he could not safely go home again? How do such circumstances affect identity and sense of self?
10. How did Suleiman's religious training shape his character and his understanding of the world?
11. Discuss the notion of storytelling woven throughout the book. How are the characters influenced by Scheherazade and *A Thousand and One Nights*? How would you characterize the storytelling style of Suleiman's mother? How does a book—Baba's lone, dangerous tome saved from the fire—drive the plot of Hisham Matar's book?

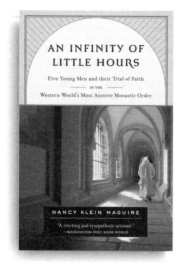

AN INFINITY OF LITTLE HOURS

Five Young Men and Their Trial of Faith in the Western World's Most Austere Monastic Order

AUTHOR: *Nancy Klein Maguire*

PUBLISHER: PublicAffairs, April 2007

WEBSITE: www.nancykleinmaguire.com

AVAILABLE IN:

Paperback, 272 pages, $13.95
ISBN 978-1-58648-432-3

Hardcover, 272 pages, $26.00
ISBN 978-1-58648-327-2

SUBJECTS: Faith/Inspiration/
Coming of Age (Memoir)

"A riveting and sympathetic account." —Washington Post Book World

"It is fascinating to enter, if only for a few hours, into this way of life, where extreme devotion forms at least a bit of a bulwark against humanity's digressions." —Los Angeles Times Book Review

SUMMARY: In 1960, five young men arrived at the imposing gates of Parkminster, the largest center of the most rigorous and ascetic monastic order in the Western world: the Carthusians. This is the story of their five-year journey into a society virtually unchanged in its behavior and lifestyle since its foundation in 1084. *An Infinity of Little Hours* is a uniquely intimate portrait of the customs and practices of a monastic order almost entirely unknown until now. It is also a drama of the men's struggle as they avoid the 1960s—the decade of hedonism, music, fashion, and amorality—and enter an entirely different era and a spiritual world of their own making. After five years, each must face a choice: to make "solemn profession" and never leave Parkminster; or to turn his back on his life's ambition to find God in solitude.

ABOUT THE AUTHOR: **Nancy Klein Maguire** is the author of numerous publications on the relationship of theatre and politics in the seventeenth century. She frequently reviews books, most recently for the *Los Angeles Times Book Review*. She has been a Scholar-in-Residence at the Folger Shakespeare Library in Washington, D.C., since 1983.

1. Were the descriptions of the monks and their lives what you expected? Were the types of people who decided to become monks those whom you would expect?

2. What do you think were the novices' motivations for pursuing the monastic life? Were other factors, besides religion, involved?

3. Which people did you think were going to "make it" to solemn profession? Were you surprised by those who were actually professed?

4. The monks, just like the rest of the world, seem not to be without their prejudices. What kind of prejudices do they have? Are they different from those of the outside world? How do you think these prejudices arise?

5. What do you think of the concepts of exclusivity and resistance to change in religious orders? Is it a good or bad thing?

6. What do you think of Dom Joseph's approach to his novitiate? Do you think that he was a good novice master? What does Maguire seem to think?

7. How do politics and hierarchy affect the character of Charterhouse life? Novices must be "voted in" to be solemnly professed. Do you think this is a fair system?

8. Why do you think that reading (as opposed to discussion) is considered such an important part of a Carthusian monk's life?

9. The Carthusians always resisted intrusions from the outside world, yet they invited Maguire into their world, and recently allowed filmmaker Phillip Gröning to make a documentary (Into Great Silence) about them. Why do you think they have lately opened their doors to outsiders?

10. Could you see yourself entering such a monastery? What would you find the hardest part about being a Carthusian monk?

11. Is there a need for this type of religious order in the world today?

12. Is there any question you would like to ask these young men, now in their senior years?

*Please visit www.readinggroupchoices.com/interviews/maguire.cfm
to see a fascinating interview with Nancy Klein Maguire.*

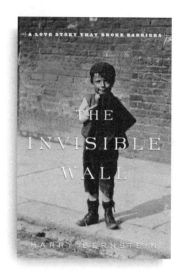

THE INVISIBLE WALL
A Love Story that Broke Barriers

AUTHOR: *Harry Bernstein*

PUBLISHER: Ballantine Books,
February 2008

WEBSITE: www.thereaderscircle.com

AVAILABLE IN:
Paperback, 336 pages, $14.95
ISBN: (13) 978-0-345-49610-2
ISBN: (10) 0-345-49610-8

SUBJECT: Coming of Age/History/Family
(Memoir)

"[A] heart-wrenching memoir . . . that brilliantly illuminates a time, a place and a family struggling valiantly to beat impossible odds." —The New York Times

"Remarkable . . . invites comparisons to Angela's Ashes.*" —USA Today*

SUMMARY: On the eve of World War I, in a small English mill town, Harry Bernstein's family struggles to make ends meet. Harry's father earns little money at the Jewish tailoring shop and brings home even less, preferring to spend his wages drinking and gambling. Harry's mother, devoted to her children and fiercely resilient, survives on her dreams: new shoes for young Harry, her daughter's marriage to the local rabbi. Then Harry's older sister does the unthinkable: She falls in love with a Christian boy. But they are separated by an "invisible wall" that divides Jewish families on one side of the street from Christian families on the other. When Harry unwittingly discovers the secret affair, he must choose between the morals he's been taught all his life, his loyalty to his selfless mother, and what he knows to be true in his own heart.

ABOUT THE AUTHOR: Ninety-seven-year-old **Harry Bernstein** emigrated to the United States with his family after World War I. He has written all his life but started writing *The Invisible Wall* only after the death of his wife, Ruby. Bernstein lives in Brick, New Jersey, and has just completed a sequel, *The Dream*, which will be published by Ballantine in summer 2008.

1. Harry Bernstein published his first memoir in his nineties; what are your own dreams, and how does Bernstein's story inspire you to reach for them?

2. Harry's mother is a remarkable woman. Her selfless acts sustain the impoverished family, and yet she disowns her daughter for marrying a Christian boy. Discuss this seeming contradiction in her character, and how she ultimately reconciles it within her own heart.

3. If you were in young Harry's position, would you have kept Lilly's love affair a secret? What was at stake for Harry in maintaining his silence?

4. Harry's sister Ruby dreams of one day having a parlor and a piano; why does she consider her mother's faded fruit shop to be a betrayal?

5. Despite all that divides them, there is a level of everyday mutual dependence linking the Jews and Christians of Bernstein's street—gaps in the invisible wall, so to speak. What examples of this mutual dependence can you think of, and do they work to dismantle the wall or to reinforce it?

6. Religious prejudice is just one of the invisible walls dividing the street and society described by Bernstein. What are some of the others, and how do these various divisions affect people on both sides of the street?

7. Are the Jews in *The Invisible Wall* guilty of prejudice against the anti-Semites surrounding them?

8. What lessons does *The Invisible Wall* have to teach about religious co-existence post-9/11, both here in America and in the world at large?

9. By encouraging Lily to improve herself through education, is her mother sowing the seeds that ultimately lead to Lily's dissatisfaction with the boundaries of Judaism and her involvement with her Christian neighbor, Arthur?

10. Why do you think Lily's father prevents her from going to the grammar school after she's won the scholarship?

11. How might *The Invisible Wall* be different if it were taking place today and, instead of Jews and Christians, the street were divided between Jews and Muslims? Sunnis and Shiites? Blacks and whites? Republicans and Democrats?

12. What does America represent to the Bernstein family?

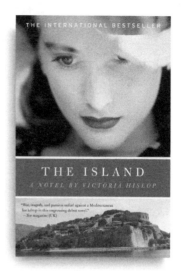

THE ISLAND

AUTHOR: *Victoria Hislop*

PUBLISHER: Harper, July 2007

WEBSITE: www.victoriahislop.com
www.harpercollins.com

AVAILABLE IN:
Paperback, 480 pages, $14.95
ISBN: 978-0-06-142926-2

SUBJECT: Family/Women's Lives
(Fiction)

"At last—a beach book with heart . . . packed with family sagas, doomed love affairs, and devastating secrets." — ***The Observer*** **(England)**

"A page-turning tale that reminds us that love and life continue in even the most extraordinary of circumstances." —***Sunday Express*** **(London)**

SUMMARY: The Petrakis family lives in Plaka, a small coastal village in Greece. Just off its coast is a tiny island called Spinalonga, home to a former leper colony, which haunts the four generations of women we meet in *The Island*. They include Eleni, who is ripped from her husband and two young daughters and sent to Spinalonga in 1939; Alexis, Eleni's great-granddaughter who visits Greece today to unlock her family's past; and Eleni's two daughters, Maria and Anna, who are as different as fire and ice and whose story is at the heart of *The Island*. In this enchanting novel their lives and loves are uncovered against the backdrop of World War II, and leprosy's touch on their family unravels the secrets they've desperately tried to keep.

ABOUT THE AUTHOR: **Victoria Hislop** writes travel features for *The Sunday Telegraph* and *The Mail* on Sunday, along with celebrity profiles for *Woman & Home*. She lives in Kent, England, with her husband and their two children.

1. How does the island of Spinalonga compare to its nearest neighbor, Plaka, in terms of natural resources and amenities?

2. How is life with leprosy portrayed in *The Island*? To what extent does it differ from any prior knowledge about the disease that you may have had?

3. What enables Eleni Petrakis to endure the separation from her family that she faces as an exile on Spinalonga?

4. How would you compare Anna and Maria's temperaments as young children, and how do their personalities affect their relationship as adults?

5. How does Anna's initial encounter with her husband's cousin, Manoli Vandoulakis, anticipate the nature of their extramarital relationship?

6. In what ways does Fortini Davaras serve as the character who links past, present, and future in the story that unfolds in *The Island?*

7. How would you characterize Maria's feelings for Dr. Kyritsis? Why is the nature of their relationship something that must be kept secret from the other residents of Spinalonga?

8. Why is Ed resistant to Alexis's need to know more about her family's past, and why does learning the truth about her mother's childhood help Alexis to make decisions regarding her relationship with Ed?

9. Why does Alexis's journey to Plaka enable Sofia to reveal aspects of her past that she had previously kept shrouded in secrecy?

10. How does leprosy connect with secrecy in the Petrakis family, and how does illness serve as a larger metaphor for the characters in *The Island?*

KABUL BEAUTY SCHOOL
An American Woman Goes Behind the Veil

AUTHORS: ***Deborah Rodriguez* with *Kristin Ohlson***

PUBLISHER: Random House Trade Paperbacks, December 2007

WEBSITE: www.thereaderscircle.com
www.oasisrecsue.org

AVAILABLE IN:
Paperback, 304 pages, $14.95
ISBN: (13) 978-0-8129-7673-1
ISBN: (10) 0-8129-7673-8

SUBJECT: Women's Lives/Inspiration/Cultural & World Issues (Memoir)

New Chapter Included in Trade Paperback Edition

"Fascinating . . . lively and honest." —*USA Today*

SUMMARY: Soon after the fall of the Taliban, in 2001, Deborah Rodriguez went to Afghanistan as part of a group offering humanitarian aid to this war-torn nation. Rodriguez, a hairdresser and mother of two from Michigan, despaired of being of any real use. But soon, she was eagerly sought out by Westerners and by Afghan women, who have a long and proud tradition of running their own beauty salons. Thus an idea was born.

With the help of corporate and international sponsors, the Kabul Beauty School welcomed its first class in 2003. Although she encountered many challenges, Rodriguez learned to empower her students to become their families' breadwinners by learning the fundamentals of coloring techniques, haircutting, and makeup.

Within the haven of the beauty school, these vibrant women shared with Rodriguez their stories and their hearts. *Kabul Beauty School* is a remarkable tale of an extraordinary community of women who come together and learn the arts of perms, friendship, and freedom.

ABOUT THE AUTHOR: **Deborah Rodriguez** has been as a hairdresser since 1979. She currently directs the Kabul Beauty School, the first modern beauty academy and training salon in Afghanistan. Rodriguez also owns the Oasis Salon and the Cabul Coffee House. She lives in Kabul with her Afghan husband.

1. We so often think of ourselves as more socially advanced than Middle Eastern nations. What does it say about this assumption that the author was treated by a preacher husband in the US the same way that Nahhida, wife of a Taliban member, is treated in Afghanistan?

2. Were you shocked when she revealed that her husband had another wife?

3. Why do you think Debbie was so emotional upon meeting Sam's father? Would you have been eager to meet him or preferred not to? Were you surprised at his reaction?

4. As a mother of two, was Debbie irresponsible in taking risks like crossing the Khyber pass and confronting her neighbors? Should she have gone to Afghanistan at all, knowing the conditions in the country?

5. Debbie's "bad" neighbors were potentially dangerous. What would you have done in her situation? How would the ineffectiveness of the local police have made you feel?

6. Was it foolish for Debbie to continue running the beauty school in the face of government interference and hostility?

7. Debbie goes to Afghanistan in order to change the lives of women there and give them greater power in their personal lives, a mission that she has fulfilled for many women. How have these women changed her?

8. Does the example of a strong self-sufficient woman Debbie sets for the Afghan women provide them with helpful inspiration, or does it set a dangerous precedent, encouraging them to model behaviors and aspirations that might be dangerous to them in their environment?

9. Would you have let a known Taliban member, and opium addict at that, stay under your roof in order to help his wife? How dangerous do you think this decision really was?

10. Why do you think Hama was unable to follow through and accept the generous offer of a place to live and a new life in the U.S.?

11. How do you think American women are similar to and, at the same time, different from the Afghan women Debbie befriended and works with?

THE KNITTING CIRCLE

AUTHOR: *Ann Hood*

PUBLISHER: W. W. Norton, January 2007

WEBSITE: www.wwnorton.com
www.annhood.us

AVAILABLE IN:
Hardcover, 384 pages, $24.95
ISBN: (13) 978-0-393-05901-4
ISBN: (10) 0-393-05901-4

SUBJECT: Family/Women's Lives/
Personal Challenges (Fiction)

"One can only admire Hood for the effort she makes in this book to describe an insupportable grief. . . . The lesson—that by being willing to share our stories, we learn how to live—cannot be dismissed." —**The Boston Globe**

"Hood's attention to craft and her experience as a novelist—and journalist—makes for an intelligent, moving read in which knitting is the tie that binds these women together and helps them to heal. Hood also brings her personal experience to the novel and transforms a life-changing event into art." —**Pages Magazine**

SUMMARY: A novel about friendship and redemption in the spirit of *How to Make an American Quilt* and *The Joy Luck Club*. After the sudden loss of her only child, Stella, Mary Baxter joins a knitting circle in Providence, Rhode Island, as a way to fill the empty hours and lonely days, not knowing that it will change her life. The women welcome Mary into their circle despite her reluctance to open her heart to them. Each woman teaches Mary a new knitting technique, and, as they do, they reveal to her their own personal stories of loss, love, and hope. Eventually, Mary is finally able to tell her own story of grief, and in so doing reclaims her love for her husband, and finds the spark of life again. By an "engrossing storyteller," this new novel once again "works its magic" (Sue Monk Kidd).

ABOUT THE AUTHOR: **Ann Hood** is the author of seven novels and a short-story collection, *An Ornithologist's Guide to Life*. She lives in Providence, Rhode Island.

1. "Time heals all wounds." So goes an old saying. How does time affect the process of mourning as witnessed in the lives of the women in *The Knitting Circle*?

2. What is it about knitting that makes the activity so therapeutic?

3. Describe the different reactions to loss experienced by the various characters in the novel. What do they hold in common? What makes each individual's situation unique?

4. Mary frequently reacts to others with feelings of envy and bitterness at their good fortune, from Beth to Jessica. What insecurities on Mary's part are revealed in her interactions with other characters in the novel?

5. Is Mary too self-indulgent when it comes to emerging from her grief?

6. Describe the importance of forgiveness in the healing processes of the characters in *The Knitting Circle*.

7. Why does it take so long for Mamie to open up to her daughter about her earlier difficulties in life? Is she entirely to blame for her reticence, or is Mary partly responsible as well?

8. How is Mary's troubled relationship with Mamie manifested in her grief over Stella?

9. How does Mary and Dylan's understanding of the bond of marriage evolve over the course of the novel?

10. Why doesn't Mary's relationship with Connor last?

11. In times of distress, Mary's impulse is often to avoid others. What is the appeal of not discussing our emotional difficulties?

12. How important is it to the women at Big Alice's Sit and Knit that theirs is a female-dominated knitting circle?

13. How are the boundaries of family redefined for Mary in the years after Stella's death?

14. Toward the end of *The Knitting Circle*, how is Mary's involvement with Holly's baby different from what it might have been at the novel's beginning?

15. Does Mary's recounting of Stella's death before her friends signify her full recovery from her loss? What more healing remains to be done after the novel's close?

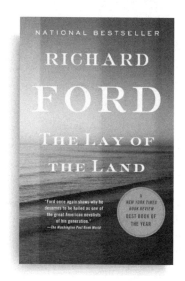

THE LAY OF THE LAND

AUTHOR: *Richard Ford*

PUBLISHER: Vintage Books, July 2007

WEBSITE: www.ReadingGroupCenter.com

AVAILABLE IN:
Paperback, 496 pages, $14.95
ISBN: 978-0-679-77667-3

SUBJECT: Family/Relationships/
Personal Challenges (Fiction)

National Book Critics Circle Award Finalist
A *New York Times Book Review* Best Book of the Year

"Ford once again shows why he deserves to be hailed as one of the great American fiction novelists of his generation." —**The Washington Post Book World**

"His intense imagination, his unwavering attention to detail, the humane spirit with which he portrays his characters and his deep interest and understanding of his times, our times, make Ford's work essential literature." —**The Atlanta Journal Constitution**

SUMMARY: A sportswriter and a real estate agent, husband and father—Frank Bascombe has been many things to many people. His uncertain youth behind him, we follow him through three days during the autumn of 2000, when his trade as a realtor on the Jersey Shore is thriving. But as a presidential election hangs in the balance, and a postnuclear-family Thanksgiving looms before him, Frank discovers that what he terms "the Permanent Period" is fraught with unforeseen perils. An astonishing meditation on America today and filled with brilliant insights, *The Lay of the Land* is a magnificent achievement from one of the most celebrated chroniclers of our time.

ABOUT THE AUTHOR: **Richard Ford** is the author of five earlier novels and three collections of stories. Ford was awarded the Pulitzer Prize and the PEN/Faulkner Award for *Independence Day*, the first book to win both prizes. In 2001 he received the PEN/Malamud Award for excellence in short fiction.

1. What do you make of the story that opens the novel: that of the community college teacher who, before being gunned down by one of her disgruntled students, was asked if she was ready to meet her maker and replied "Yes. Yes, I think I am." Why is Frank so riveted by this question? How does he think he might answer in similar circumstances?

2. *The Lay of the Land* is set during Thanksgiving, as *The Sportswriter* takes place at Easter and *Independence Day* over a July 4th weekend. How does the holiday figure in the novel? How does Frank feel about it, and how do the other characters appear to be celebrating it? Discuss the novel's exploration of themes like gratitude, family, and abundance —as well as the ambiguous meaning of "pilgrim."

3. What is the significance of Frank's career as a realtor? Which of his character traits does it bring into relief? How does it cause him to see the landscape and houses around him, and how does it cause other characters to see him? What does "home" mean to a realtor, who makes his living selling them?

4. Frank is a cancer survivor, a category whose ambiguity may be surpassed only by the "suicide survivors" that so confuse Mike. How does Frank feel about his condition, and particularly about where it has chosen to turn up in his body?

5. As its title suggests, *The Lay of the Land* is very much a novel about place. How does Bascombe view his neck of New Jersey? How do his observations about strip malls, McMansions, road houses, and human tissue banks illuminate Bascombe's character? How do they comment on the novel's action? Does Bascombe loathe the uniformity and ugliness of this environment, or are his feelings about them more complex?

6. Frank is both the novel's protagonist and its narrator. Every perception and event is filtered through his voice. How would you characterize Frank's voice? In what ways does it combine the casual and the literary, the comic and the tragic?

For the complete Reading Group Guide,
visit www.ReadingGroupCenter.com.

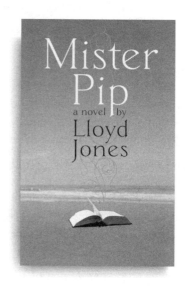

MISTER PIP

AUTHOR: *Lloyd Jones*

PUBLISHER: Dial Press, September 2007

WEBSITE: www.dialpress.com
www.misterpip.com

AVAILABLE IN:
Hardcover, 256 pages, $20.00
ISBN: (13) 978-0-385-34106-6
ISBN: (10) 0-385-341067

SUBJECT: Family/Faith/Identity (Fiction)

Winner 2007 Commonwealth Prize for Best Book

"Jones's prose is faultless. . . . With a mixture of thrill and unease, Matilda discovers independent thought, and Jones captures the intricate, emotionally loaded evolution of the mother-daughter relationship." —**Publishers Weekly**

"The novel is a paean to the transformative power of literature, particularly its ability to occlude an unpleasant reality with a fictional alternative and to expand an individual's sense of possibility." —**New York Sun**

SUMMARY: *Mister Pip* unites the stirring tale of a young girl's quest for hope with a marvelous tribute to a Charles Dickens classic. Thirteen-year-old Matilda is coming of age on a Pacific island that has been torn apart by war. Almost everyone, including her father, has left to find work or escape the danger. Among those who stayed behind is the eccentric and mysterious Mr. Watts, the sole remaining white man, who becomes a teacher and begins to read *Great Expectations* aloud to the students. For Matilda and her classmates, the story offers an escape from their brutal reality, while instilling in them the strength to endure in a place where nothing is certain. In this gripping and imaginative novel, Lloyd Jones gives us a unique way to explore issues of faith, family, loyalty, identity, and, ultimately, the transcendence of literature.

ABOUT THE AUTHOR: **Lloyd Jones**'s previous novels and collections of stories include the award-winning *The Book of Fame, Biografi*, a *New York Times* Notable Book, *Choo Woo, Here at the End of the World We Learn to Dance* and *Paint Your Wife*. Lloyd Jones lives in Wellington, New Zealand.

1. Is it important that Mr. Watts is the last white man on the island? Why?
2. Why does Matilda write Pip's name in the sand alongside the names of her relatives? How does this contribute to Dolores's feelings about Mr. Watts's instruction of her daughter? Are these feelings understandable?
3. What is the message Matilda's mother is trying to express to the children with the story of her mother's braids? How is this related to the issue of Mr. Watts's faith in God?
4. Discuss how the characters in this story struggle to reconcile the concepts of race and identity. How does it influence their concepts of self? What moments, especially, helped reveal this to you?
5. Why does Dolores step forward to declare herself "God's witness" to the murder of Mr. Watts? Were you surprised that she did? Why does she insist that Matilda remain silent?
6. Discuss your memorable experiences of being read to as a child. What book made the greatest impact on your life? Did any book come to you at precisely the right time, the way *Great Expectations* was brought to Matilda?
7. Are both *Mister Pip* and *Great Expectations* universal coming-of-age tales? How did you react to the blending of these two distinctly different settings and time periods?
8. The initial lines of *Great Expectations* are reflected several times in this novel. Compare them to the opening lines of *Mister Pip*. What connections do these first sentences draw between the themes of both novels?
9. In what way are the narrative voices of *Mister* Pip and *Great Expectations* the same? How are they different? What shifts do you notice in the storytelling after Matilda leaves the island? How did this impact your reading?
10. How is Dolores's treatment of Matilda similar to Estella's treatment of Pip in *Great Expectations*? How does this relationship help Matilda understand Pip's attachment to Estella? Is it necessary that this attachment be severed before Pip/Matilda can grow individually?
11. Why do you think Mr. Watts omitted the characters of Orlick and Compeyson from his telling of *Great Expectations*?
12. What is signified by the changing of one's name, both in *Great Expectations* and *Mister Pip*? Why does Matilda not change her name?
13. In what ways does *Great Expectations* help Matilda cope with her reality and prepare her for the future? How does it help Mr. Watts deal with his past? What makes *Great Expectations* the ideal Dickens choice for this purpose?

MY LATEST GRIEVANCE

AUTHOR: *Elinor Lipman*

PUBLISHER: Mariner Books, May 2007

WEBSITE: www.marinerbooks.com
www.elinorlipman.com

AVAILABLE IN:
Paperback, 256 pages, $13.95
ISBN: (13) 978-0-618-87235-0
ISBN: (10) 0-618-87235-3

SUBJECT: Humor/Relationships/Identity
(Fiction)

Selected as a Best Book of the Year — *Washington Post*
A *New York Times* **Editor's Choice and A Book Sense Notable**

"It is very rare you get to read a book that holds you enchanted on every page, but Lipman's latest casts just that spell." —**Nigella Lawson**

"Turn Lipman loose on conflicting moralities and shifting allegiances, and you always will be entertained." —**Miami Herald**

"So entertaining you're sorry to see it end." —**Seattle Times**

SUMMARY: *My Latest Grievance* stars the beguiling teenager Frederica Hatch, the "Eloise of Dewing College." Born and raised in the dormitory of this small women's college and chafing under the care of "the most annoyingly evenhanded parental team in the history of civilization," Frederica is starting to feel that her life is stiflingly snug. That all changes with the arrival on campus of a new dorm mother, the glamorous Laura Lee French, the frenetic center of her own universe.

ABOUT THE AUTHOR: **Elinor Lipman** is the author of seven previous novels, including *The Pursuit of Alice Thrift*, *The Inn at Lake Devine*, *The Ladies' Man*, *Isabel's Bed*, and *Then She Found Me*. Four of her novels have been optioned for film and are in various stages of development. She divides her time between Northampton, Massachusetts, and New York City. In 2001 she won the New England Booksellers Award for fiction. She has taught at Simmons, Hampshire, and Smith colleges, which bear no resemblance to Dewing.

1. The book is narrated by the adult Frederica Hatch as she looks back at a tumultuous teenage year. Does the author make the combined sensibility—age sixteen viewed through the eyes of the narrator's present self—work?

2. Why do you think the author made Dewing a lackluster institution rather than a top-notch college?

3. Frederica asks on page 1, "Were they types, my parents-to-be? From a distance and for a long time, it appeared to be so." Does this serve as a warning? A prediction? A wink from the author? An apology?

4. Laura Lee French's ex-husband is a distant cousin. Would the story have unfolded in the same way if she had not been a relative?

5. Marietta Woodbury and her mother are rude to Laura Lee upon first speaking to her on campus. Did this meeting resonate with you and signal *trouble ahead*?

6. The professors Hatch are passionately committed to righting wrongs and to each other. In what ways do they let their daughter down?

7. What turning point triggers Frederica's more sympathetic and respectful view of her parents?

8. One could say that the Blizzard of '78 is a character in *My Latest Grievance*. Did the author succeed in conveying the power of that historic storm and effectively put you there?

9. Did you find any character less than fully developed? What else did you want to know about him or her?

10. Laura Lee French, narcissist extraordinaire: is it possible to feel sympathy for this character?

11. Chapter 33, "Emeriti," the epilogue, brings the reader to the present. How well does the jump forward in time wrap up the story?

THE NIGHT JOURNAL

AUTHOR: **Elizabeth Crook**

PUBLISHER: Penguin Books, February 2007

WEBSITE: www.elizabethcrookbooks.com

AVAILABLE IN:
Paperback, 464 pages, $14.00
ISBN: (13) 978-0-143-03857-3
ISBN: (10) 0-14-303857-5

SUBJECT: Family/Identity/
American History (Fiction)

". . . warmly drawn . . . delightful reading . . . A multilayered narrative of impressive historical perspicacity, enriched by the author's loving attention to character." —**Kirkus Reviews**

"The Night Journal *is Austin novelist Elizabeth Crook's first book in more than a decade, but the epic tale spanning a century of family history is worth the wait. Ms. Crook's prose is elegant, and her novel is a page-turner.* The Night Journal *more than meets my personal standard for quality fiction: When I finished, I wished there were more."* —**Dallas Morning News**

"Crook has a clear gift for detail and dialogue. . . . [T]here's plenty to keep you engaged and engrossed." —**The Philadelphia Inquirer**

SUMMARY: Both a fascinating historical epic of the Southwest and a searing personal story of one family's coming to terms with its own past, *The Night Journal* is a contemporary love story and a historical mystery, depicting the conflict between cultures in New Mexico at the turn of the last century, between sexes both then and now, and inevitably the conflicts between generations. It is centered on the mystery of the contents buried in a dog's grave, but the underlying, broader mystery is about connections between the past and the present and the ways in which people relate to their ancestors both in life and in legacy.

ABOUT THE AUTHOR: **Elizabeth Crook** is the author of two previous novels and has been published in anthologies and periodicals such as *Texas Monthly* and *Southwestern Historical Quarterly*. She has devoted most of the last decade to researching and writing this book.

1. How important is it in our contemporary lives to feel a connection to the past or to have an understanding of our ancestors? Are the stories about your ancestors important to your own self-image?

2. Are we, as a generation, pale in comparison to our ancestors, as Meg seems to believe? In other words, do we lack their strength? Are there ways in which we are stronger?

3. Bassie essentially raised both Nina and Meg. Why did her overbearing personality affect them so differently? Are some children more genetically inclined to survive bad parenting?

4. Many of the central characters—Bassie, Elliott, Jim, and even Meg —are in some respects orphans. What does it mean to be an orphan? How does being orphaned affect a person's connection to the world around them?

5. Which of the historical male characters are you more drawn to— Elliott Bass or Vicente Morales? Which one do you respect more?

6. Is your respect for Hannah diminished by the ultimate revelation of her affair with Vicente? Do you think you, as a reader, are more forgiving of, and less judgmental about, extramarital affairs between historical characters than you are of those between contemporary characters?

7. Do you believe Meg and Jim are soul mates, kept apart through circumstance, or are they merely swept up in the drama of Hannah and Elliott's story?

8. Are you relieved that Meg ultimately resists having an affair with Jim, or would you feel more satisfied if she had allowed the relationship to go further? In general do you prefer, in literature, to be gratified or left slightly unsatisfied? Do you feel that stories, and perhaps even real-life stories, are richer if a deep love affair is left somewhat unrealized, or if it is fully satisfied?

9. Given Meg's personality, do you think she matures and changes enough in the course of the book that her future will be different from what it would have been had she not gone to New Mexico with Bassie?

10. Meg and Jim are surprised by several discoveries in the last third of the novel. Which of these discoveries took you by surprise as a reader and which did you anticipate?

11. Were you ultimately more engaged by Meg's story or by Hannah's? Which did you find yourself most eager to return to while reading, and most reluctant to leave?

NO! I DON'T WANT TO JOIN A BOOK CLUB

Diary of a 60th Year

AUTHOR: *Virginia Ironside*

PUBLISHER: Plume Books, March 2008

WEBSITE: us.penguingroup.com
www.virginiaironside.org

AVAILABLE IN:

Paperback, 240 pages, $14.00
ISBN: (13) 978-0-452-28923-9
ISBN: (10) 0-45-228923-8

SUBJECT: Humor/Women's Lives/
Coming of Age (Fiction)

"This screamingly funny memoir is for your world-weary gal pals. And possibly yourself." —USA TODAY

"I'm thinking of reading No! I Don't Want to Join a Book Club *once a year here on in to cheer myself up. If you're over 50, you should read it, too." —The Buffalo News*

SUMMARY: Marie Sharp, a child of the 1960s, is entering her own 60s. Behind her is a life full of experiences. She has been known to be reckless and irresponsible, at least by today's standards. Now she's old and wants to feel that way.

In *No! I Don't Want to Join a Book Club*, Marie swears off all kinds of things that her friends and contemporaries are embracing. Her friends may see her as a contrarian, but she shocks everyone when she declares she is swearing off men. Forever. But amid the simple pleasures Marie craves are real complications she cannot ignore. Some of those dearest to her may not be around to grow old along with her. She must realize that no matter what life one chooses, embraces, or is given, it has only one possible ending.

Still, maybe there are more possibilities ahead for her than she allows herself to dream—or to admit to her diary. Perhaps, even for Marie, this new stage in life won't turn out quite according to her simple plan.

ABOUT THE AUTHOR: **Virginia Ironside** is a journalist, agony aunt, and author, divorced living in West London. She has one son and one grandson.

1. Marie talks about "longing to feel sixty." Does she really want this—and what does feeling one's age mean anyway?
2. In what ways does Marie defy popular notions of older people, especially older women? In what ways does she (wittingly or unwittingly) conform to them?
3. What role do Hughie and James play in Marie's life? What does her relationship with them as a couple and with Hughie in particular give her that no one else does?
4. Why does Marie take pride in the achievement of reaching sixty but feel no urge to try to achieve anything new?
5. Marie is critical of the way many women her age appear asexual, yet she makes a big deal of swearing off men and sex for the rest of her life—leading an asexual lifestyle, as it were. Does she mean it? What's behind her determination? Is giving up something she doesn't have really a sacrifice or does it mean something else?
6. We know what Marie thinks of other sixtysomethings' efforts to try new things and otherwise attempt to make themselves feel (and look) young and attractive—Penny, for example. But what might Penny think of Marie's attitude?
7. "How many other characters can I expect to be before I die?" wonders Marie. Earlier she has mentioned seeing her older self and her younger self as distinct from each other. Later, she and Hughie agree that people are made up of many "real selves" that are often in conflict with one another. How does this come through in the character of Marie? Does she surprise us (and herself)? Does she see other people as having multiple selves?
8. Hughie seems to face his end in a matter-of-fact way, including explaining to Marie how good it feels to be free of all the choices and pressures of really old age. How does this compare with Marie's attitude about aging? Is she in denial herself?
9. How does the time in which Marie and her contemporaries were young adults (the reckless, tumultuous 1960s) affect the way they face getting older? Why is someone like Philippa's sister, who speaks to Marie of "our age," different?
10. In theory, Marie confides all to her diary, writing her most private thoughts with candor. But in practice, does she?
11. If Marie could be persuaded to join a book club, what kind of member would she be? How would she contribute? How would she get along with other members?

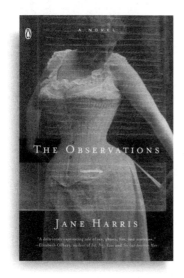

THE OBSERVATIONS

AUTHOR: *Jane Harris*

PUBLISHER: Penguin Books, June 2007

WEBSITE: us.penguingroup.com

AVAILABLE IN:
Paperback, 416 pages, $14.00
ISBN: 978-0-14-311201-3

SUBJECT: Identity/Women's Lives/
Culture & World Issues (Fiction)

Finalist for the Orange Broadband Prize for Fiction

"Bessy Buckley can hold her head up with Moll Flanders and Becky Sharp as a living, breathing mortal. . . . What one takes away is [her] earthy voice, clear as a bell, ringing out her tale of love, loss and redemption."
—The Times (London)

"It's a rare feeling to be swept up by a book in the childhood way, but when it happens, it's extraordinary: deeply familiar and strangely unsettling." —The London Review of Books

"By turns funny and sad, but always true to the ear. And the sprightly, profane Bessy is a joy." —Entertainment Weekly

SUMMARY: *The Observations* is a hugely assured and darkly funny debut set in nineteenth-century Scotland. Bessy Buckley, the novel's heroine, is a cynical, wide-eyed, and tender fifteen-year-old Irish girl who takes a job as a maid in a once-grand country house outside Edinburgh, where all is not as it seems. Asked by her employer, the beautiful Arabella, to keep a journal of her most intimate thoughts, Bessy soon makes a troubling discovery and realizes that she has fled her difficult past only to arrive in an even more disturbing present.

ABOUT THE AUTHOR: **Jane Harris**'s short stories have appeared in a wide variety of anthologies and magazines, and she has written several award-winning short films. In 2000, she received a Writer's Award from the Arts Council of England.

1. How does Bessy's and her mistress' enormous difference in social status shape their relationship? Do they ever truly overcome this gap, and if so, at what cost?

2. What is Arabella Reid's view of the working classes before Bessy's arrival? Does her acquaintance with Bessy change Arabella's view of her supposed inferiors, and if so, how?

3. Arabella is virtually obsessed with chronicling and analyzing the thoughts and actions of her maidservants. How would you characterize the motives behind her research? Is her interest propelled by kindness, aggression, voyeurism, or some other emotional or intellectual force?

4. How does Arabella perceive Bessy in her secret manuscript, and how does the novel as a whole challenge and correct Arabella's "observations" on this point?

5. Although they never meet, Bessy and Nora are implicitly compared throughout the novel, with Nora being represented as the good girl and Bessy figuring as the bad one. Despite these implied designations, however, it is Nora who is destroyed by sexual mistreatment, whereas Bessy survives and achieves a degree of triumph over her past. What accounts for this difference in outcome?

6. At the end of the novel, Arabella announces that her new magnum opus will treat the subject of insanity. However, she comments to Bessy that this work is "barely begun." Few if any of the characters in *The Observations* are free from some kind of obsession or emotional disturbance. Choose a character other than Arabella and offer an analysis of her or his mental health.

7. Early in the novel, Bessy is resistant to Arabella's command that she write about everything that befalls her. At the end of the novel, however, we learn that she has written the entire story we have just read at the behest of Dr. Lawrence, who, like Arabella before him, takes a clinical interest in her "observations." Why and how do you think Bessy has so completely overcome her reluctance to express herself?

8. How do women in the novel deal with the demands of masculine self-interest? In what instances are their responses successful, and why?

9. Throughout *The Observations*, Bessy makes judgments about her own character and actions. In this novel, in which analysis and surveillance take place everywhere, how accurate is Bessy when it comes to observing herself?

10. What perceptions and values are associated with Irishness in the novel? Do these perceptions remain constant, or do they vary depending on person and circumstance?

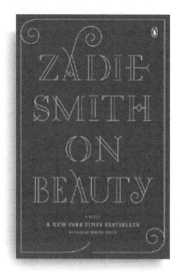

ON BEAUTY

AUTHOR: *Zadie Smith*

PUBLISHER: Penguin Books, August 2006

WEBSITE: www.penguin.com

AVAILABLE IN:
Paperback, 464 pages, $15.00
ISBN 978-0-143-03774-3

SUBJECT: Family/Relationships/
Women's Lives (Fiction)

" . . . *[A] thoroughly original tale about families and generational change, about race and multiculturalism in millennial America, about love and identity and the ways they are affected by the passage of time. . . . A novel that is as affecting as it is entertaining, as provocative as it is humane.*"
—**Michiko Kakutani, *The New York Times***

"*As good as she is with big ideas, Smith is even stronger at capturing family dynamics, the heartbreak of broken trust as well as the lovely connections between siblings.*" —***The Los Angeles Times Book***

SUMMARY: Howard Belsey, a Rembrandt scholar who doesn't like Rembrandt, is an Englishman abroad and a long-suffering professor at Wellington, a liberal New England arts college. He has been married for thirty years to Kiki, an American woman who no longer resembles the sexy activist she once was. Their three children passionately pursue their own paths. An infidelity, a death, and a legacy set in motion a chain of events that sees all parties forced to examine the unarticulated assumptions which underpin their lives.

Set on both sides of the Atlantic, Zadie Smith's third novel is a brilliant analysis of family life, the institution of marriage, intersections of the personal and political, and an honest look at people's deceptions. It is also, as you might expect, very funny indeed.

ABOUT THE AUTHOR: **Zadie Smith** was born in northwest London in 1975 and still lives in the area. She is the author of *White Teeth* and *The Autograph Man*.

1. What are the effects of Howard's infidelity on the Kiki and his children? He and Kiki interpret the meaning of his act differently? Can you understand both sides

2. The Belsey children are all searching for an adult identity. Which of their current activities do you see as "phases" in their lives, and which do you think are meant to suggest what they will harden into as adults? Which of them do you identify with the most?

3. The Belseys' house, beautifully evoked by Smith as the calm center around which the whirlwind of family life turns, embodies the family's comfortable middle class stature. What does the home represent, both practically and emotionally, to various members of the family?

4. How do people treat Kiki, and what do both her race and size have to do with this? Do you think she is more empowered over the course of the novel, or less?

5. Why do you think that Howard feels so antagonistic toward representational beauty in art? What does this suggest about the rest of his life? Do you think he is missing something crucial about art or life?

6. Consider the various members of the two families. How would you describe each one's politics or belief system? How do they struggle to fully act on those beliefs in their daily lives? Does anyone really live true to their ideals?

7. Women's body issues recur throughout the novel. Are their bodies at all accurate representations of who they are? How do they struggle with, or come to terms with, their physical selves? Does anyone have a healthy (and sustainable) physical regard for themselves?

8. Some people have described Smith's writing as satire—that is, work that exposes human folly, offering it up for ridicule. Do you think her depictions of characters are satirical? Which characters or moments in the book transcend such stereotype? Are there characters who are both ridiculous and real?

9. The title *On Beauty* refers to many things. How does each characters express their radically different ideas about the meaning and role of beauty in their lives? What do you think it means, in this novel's terms, to embrace beauty? What does it mean to be without it? What, to Smith and to you, are truly beautiful things?

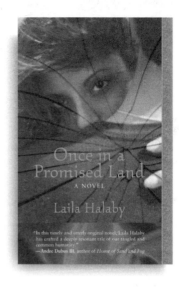

ONCE IN A PROMISED LAND

AUTHOR: *Laila Halaby*

PUBLISHER: Beacon Press, January 2008

WEBSITE: www.lailahalaby.net
www.beacon.org

AVAILABLE IN:
Paperback, 352 pages, $14.00
ISBN 978-080708391-8

ALSO AVAILABLE IN:
Hardcover, 352 pages, $23.95
ISBN 978-080708390-1

SUBJECTS: Cultural & World Issues/
Family/Personal Challenges (Fiction)

A Book Sense Notable Title

A Selection of Barnes & Noble's Discover Great New Writers Program

"Highly recommended for both public and academic libraries, this novel would make a thought-provoking book club choice."—**Library Journal**

"Halaby is spot-on in her observations of how slowly a once-idyllic union can crumble." —USA Today

SUMMARY: *Once in a Promised Land* is the story of Jassim and Salwa, who left the deserts of their native Jordan for those of Arizona, each chasing mirages of opportunity and freedom. Although the couple live far from Ground Zero, they cannot escape the dust cloud of paranoia settling over the nation. When Jassim kills a teenage boy in a terrible accident and Salwa becomes hopelessly entangled with a shadowy young American, their tenuous lives in exile and their fragile marriage begin to unravel. *Once in a Promised Land* is a dramatic and achingly honest look at what it means to straddle cultures, to be viewed with suspicion, and to struggle to find safe haven.

ABOUT THE AUTHOR: **Laila Halaby** was born in Beirut, Lebanon, to a Jordanian father and an American mother. She speaks four languages, won a Fulbright scholarship to study folklore in Jordan, and holds a master's degree in Arabic literature. Her first novel, *West of the Jordan*, won the prestigious PEN Beyond Margins Award. She lives in Tucson, Arizona, with her family.

1. Salwa and Jassim find themselves surrounded by hostility after the attacks on the World Trade Center. Did you notice a change in attitude towards Arabs in the U.S. after 9/11? Are there other groups in your community that are discriminated against because of their ethnicity or religion? Have you ever been subject to discrimination?

2. Jassim kills a teenage boy in a car accident. What would your reaction be if you hit and killed someone? Would you go visit the victim's family, as Jassim did, or avoid them? What if you were the parent of a child who was killed in an accident—would you want to meet the person who was responsible, even if accidentally, for your child's death?

3. Salwa doesn't tell Jassim that she is pregnant. Why not? How would you have handled this situation?

4. Halaby tells the story from two very different points of view: Salwa's and Jassim's. Is one of them more compelling for you, or easier to identify with? Do you find that at different times in the story you are sympathizing or siding with either Salwa or Jassim?

5. Every aspect of Jassim's life is splitting apart: he kills a boy in a car accident, he gets fired from his job as hydrologist, and his wife is becoming distant and secretive. How does he handle these three crises? If you were in his place, would you have done anything differently? Can you think of a time in your own life when you had to deal with frustrating circumstances that were outside your control?

6. Salwa's friend Randa, to whom she confesses about her affair with Jake, advises her not to tell Jassim, "no matter what." Would you have advised her differently?

7. Arab culture is an integral part of Salwa's and Jassim's identities, and even though before 9/11 their life in the U.S. is quite comfortable, it is inevitable that at times they feel misplaced and yearn for the sense of belonging and the warm familiarity of their homelands. Have you ever had to negotiate between your own culture and a foreign one?

8. When Jake cooks dinner for Salwa, he offers her candy-coated shumur (fennel), which "brought back desserts eaten only during Ramadan, brought back home in one tiny burst and then another." If you were away from your home, what would be your *shumur*?

9. What do you think happens at the end of the novel? Is Salwa dying? Are they reconciled? How do you interpret the folk tale?

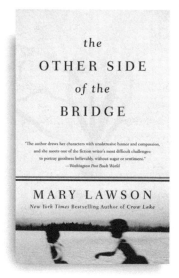

THE OTHER SIDE OF THE BRIDGE

AUTHOR: *Mary Lawson*

PUBLISHER: Dial Press, September 2007

WEBSITE: www.dialpress.com

AVAILABLE IN:
Paperback, 320 pages, $14.00
ISBN: (13) 978-0-385-34038-0
ISBN: (10) 0-385-34038-9

SUBJECT: Family/Relationship/
Coming of Age (Fiction)

"Lawson beautifully skirts the clichés of sibling rivalry embedded since Cain and Abel, with a story that aches with its inevitability and yet suggests hope." —**New York Daily News**

"[Lawson] writes vividly of the joys and hardships of rural life, the harsh but sublime beauties of the natural world, as well as the threads connecting one generation to the next and the depredations wrought by the flow of man-made history." —**Los Angeles Times**

SUMMARY: *The Other Side of the Bridge* weaves together the stories of two families as they seek solace and redemption across two generations.

Set during the 1930s against the backdrop of northern Ontario's haunting landscapes, *The Other Side of the Bridge* opens with an unforgettable image of Arthur and Jake Dunn, two brothers whose jealousies will take them beyond the edge of reason, to a deadly point of no return.When a beautiful young woman named Laura moves into their community, she propels their sibling rivalry to its breaking point.

Years later, the local doctor's son, Ian, takes a job at the Dunn farm and develops an attachment to Laura. He stumbles onto a secret that forever alters the course of Arthur's life.

ABOUT THE AUTHOR: **Mary Lawson** was born and brought up in a farming community in central Ontario. She moved to England in 1968, is married with two sons and lives in Kingston-upon-Thames. This is her second novel.

1. How were you affected by the novel's prologue? What did you discover about Arthur and Jake in this scene? How did your perceptions of the brothers change throughout the book?
2. How would you answer the questions that conclude the prologue? What accounts for the differences between those who follow the rules, like Arthur, and those who defy them? Which came more easily for you as an adolescent: obedience or defiance?
3. How were Jake and Arthur affected by their family dynamic?
4. What was the effect of the novel's timeline? How did it compare to your own experience of the continuum between present moments and memory?
5. Discuss the use of the headlines that open each chapter. What do they say about the local and global concerns of humanity? In what way were the headlines timeless, and in what way did they convey the unique attributes of this locale? What headlines would be most significant in marking the chapters of your life?
6. What is the significance of the two time periods in the lives of the characters? What dreams for the future did each of these generations possess?
7. Discuss the nature of love and marriage as described in the novel. What made Jake so irresistible to Laura? What made Dr. Christopherson's wife choose another man? What is the riskiest romantic decision you have made?
8. How are the characters shaped by the novel's setting? What separates those who want to escape from those who bask in the town's familiarity? Do you think people who grow up in cities feel the same passion for them as the characters in these two novels feel for the land?
9. Why is Ian so transformed by the "day of the dragonflies" that concludes chapter nine? What did these memories mean to him?
10. Discuss the novel's title. What does it mean for the characters to reach the other side of the bridge? Could Jake and Arthur ever be free of the wounds they inflicted on each other?
11. Who ultimately was responsible for Jake's fall from the bridge? Who ultimately paid the price (literally, in terms of his medical bills, and figuratively as well)?
12. Discuss the cycles of tragedy conveyed in the Dunn family history, from the death of Arthur's father to the closing scenes of Carter. How do characters cope with the concepts of fate versus intent? How do they cope with regret?

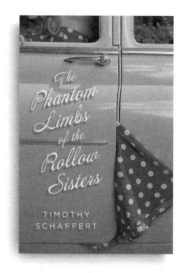

THE PHANTOM LIMBS OF THE ROLLOW SISTERS

AUTHOR: *Timothy Schaffert*

PUBLISHER: Unbridled Books, October 2007

WEBSITE: www.unbridledbooks.com

AVAILABLE IN:
Paperback, 240 pages, $14.95
ISBN: 978-1-932961-42-3

SUBJECT: Family/Relationships/
Women's Lives (Fiction)

"... *blithe, quirky ... spirited, offbeat ...*" —**Janet Maslin, *The New York Times***

"... *boondocks-Gothic ... quietly tragic. ... The sisters lose their childhood innocence only to acquire an adult version. ... As long as the sisters have each other, nothing else matters.*" —***The Washington Post***

SUMMARY: Renowned author Timothy Schaffert's celebrated debut novel chronicles two sisters on the cusp of womanhood as they struggle to understand their father's suicide as well their mother's abandonment of them many years earlier. On graduating from high school, the sisters are once again set adrift, this time by their grandmother who leaves them for Florida. In order to survive, and perhaps even thrive, on their path to adulthood, they must learn to reconcile their pasts and discover how to depend upon themselves as well as on each other.

In a story that rises out of the spare Nebraska landscape, Schaffert delivers a redemptive tale about two young women searching for wholeness and love.

ABOUT THE AUTHOR: **Timothy Schaffert** is the award-winning author of two other novels: *The Singing and Dancing Daughters of God* and *Devils in the Sugar Shack*. He lives in Nebraska, where he is the director of the (Downtown) Omaha Lit Fest and a contributing editor for the *Prairie Schooner* literary journal.

1. What do you think Lily and Mabel most need?

2. Much of this novel focuses on grief and surviving grief. Do you think, though, that it is a sad book?

3. The girls live in an isolated, rural area, and they run an antique/second hand shop. How do these places affect the story? How does Schaffert use setting to advance the tale?

4. How are men portrayed in this novel? How are families?

5. How does this novel change your perspective about Nebraska? Are books that offer perspective or challenge assumptions the kinds of books you prefer to read?

6. Why do you think Mabel starts going by the name Mabel?

7. When Lily finally meets her mother, Fiona tells Lily why they were abandoned. When she meets Ana, she learns the truth about her father's death. How do these scenes change the story? Is the truth what Lily really wanted?

8. Why does the story of Charlie Starkweather and Caril Ann Fugate hold such continued interest for us, and what does this say about Middle America?

9. Though they end up together once more, in what ways have their journeys differed, and how does their resilience offer hope for the future and a sense of redemption?

10. In some ways this story is a search for belonging. In what differing ways are the girls able to find acceptance of the past, and how does that affect their capacity for normal human relations?

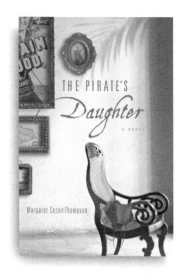

THE PIRATE'S DAUGHTER

AUTHOR: *Margaret Cezair-Thompson*

PUBLISHER: Unbridled Books, October 2007

WEBSITE: www.unbridledbooks.com

AVAILABLE IN:
Hardcover, 352 pages, $24.95
ISBN: 978-1-932961-40-9

SUBJECT: Coming of Age/Women's Lives/Culture & World Issues (Fiction)

"There are books and then there are great books. Once in awhile, these days, a great book comes along that makes a bookseller proud to be a part of its success. The Kite Runner, The Life of Pi, *and now* The Pirate's Daughter. The Pirate's Daughter *is a literary triumph that combines all the elements of a great novel: romance, intrigue, history, glamour and suspense. What an unforgettable masterpiece. I can't wait for the giant to awaken!"* **—Marva Allen, Hue-Man Bookstore (NY)**

SUMMARY: After a long and storied career on the silver screen, Errol Flynn spent much of the last years of his life on a small island off of Jamaica, throwing parties and sleeping with increasingly younger teenaged girls. Based on those years, *The Pirate's Daughter* is the story of Ida, a local girl who has an affair with Flynn that produces a daughter, May, who meets her father but once.

Spanning two generations of women whose destinies become inextricably linked with the matinee idol's, this lively novel tells the provocative history of a vanished era, of uncommon kinships, compelling attachments, betrayal and atonement in a paradisal, tropical setting

ABOUT THE AUTHOR: **Margaret Cezair-Thompson** is the author of a widely acclaimed previous novel, *The True History of Paradise*. Born in Jamaica, West Indies, she teaches literature and creative writing at Wellesley College.

1. Is this the story of a pirate's daughter? Why or why not? Is there more than one pirate in the novel?

2. How does Cezair-Thompson use the concept of pirates to tell the larger political story of Jamaica's path to independence? What does this book say about Colonialism?

3. Is this a novel about race? Is it a novel about class?

4. Passions run deep in this novel, both love and hate. Do you consider this a love story? Is it a love story between couples, or a love song for Jamaica, or both? What various kinds of love fuel the plot? What kinds of hatred drive the narrative?

5. Strong mothers abound in this book, even the mothers we read about only in passing who leave Jamaica for New York to earn a living for their children. Do you think Ida is a good mother? Do you think that is a fair question, given the challenges she faced? How important are fathers, and father figures?

6. Maps play a significant role in this novel. The greatest mysteries, though, are finding ways to understand hearts and histories. What guides May in her journey toward self-discovery? How does Nigel find peace?

7. How does the story of Errol Flynn and Hollywood add to the novel?

8. How do the interplay of fact and fiction enliven the story?

9. Place is critical in this novel. How does Cezair-Thompson use different settings to advance her tale?

10. What notions of beauty shape this story?

11. Much of the novel is about seduction, but not always the literal kind. What seduces different characters, and why?

12. Movies are important to the story, but in the end May is most influenced by words and books. Why does she seem more interested in one form of media over the other?

13. How important to the novel is the theme of forgiveness?

14. Is Jamaica a character in this novel?

PLUM WINE

AUTHOR: *Angela Davis-Gardner*

PUBLISHER: Dial Press, April 2007

WEBSITE: www.dialpress.com
www.angeladavisgardner.com

AVAILABLE IN:
Paperback, 352 pages, $13.00
ISBN: (13) 978-0-385-34083-0
ISBN: (10) 0-385-34083-4

SUBJECT: Relationships/Women's Lives/
Intrigue (Fiction)

A March 2006 Book Sense Pick

"A mystery that unfolds as beautifully, delicately, and ceremoniously as a lotus blossom. One of the most memorable novels I have read in many years." —**Lee Smith, author of *On Agate Hill***

SUMMARY: In the beautifully written, multi-layered novel *Plum Wine*, Angela Davis-Gardner portrays the love story between Seiji, a Japanese potter who endured the terrors brought about by the Hiroshima bombing, and Barbara Jefferson, a lonely young American teaching English at an all-girls Tokyo university. *Plum Wine* is set in Japan during the Vietnam War era. Barbara receives a bequest from her fellow teacher and mentor, Michi-San. Michi-San has left her a chest filled with bottles of plum wine dated each year from 1939 to the present year, 1966. Wrapped around each bottle are sheets of rice paper covered in calligraphy that reveal portions of Michi-San's and her mother's lives. As Barbara journeys through two worlds, two time periods, and two women's lives to understand the texts, she discovered a story of shame and secrets, of trust and betrayal, and the clash of civilizations.

ABOUT THE AUTHOR: **Angela Davis-Gardner** is the author of the internationally acclaimed novels *Felice* and *Forms of Shelter*. An Alumni Distinguished Professor at North Carolina State University in Raleigh, Angela has won nearly thirty awards for writing and teaching. She lives in Raleigh, North Carolina, where she is at work on her next novel.

1. Does it change the reading experience to watch history unfold from the translation of buried papers? Is this narrative approach effective?

2. Discuss the significance of a fox to the Japanese. What is so appealing about the stories about the Fox-Woman? Can Barbara be considered a fox? If so, in what ways?

3. "It was strange, she thought, how the placement of objects affected them. It was true for people too." (page 12) Sentiments of alienation engulf Barbara throughout the novel. What makes her feel so different?

4. How does learning about Michi-San, Seji, and Rie's Hiroshima experiences affect Barbara? Do their stories further distinguish her or do they make her feel more connected?

5. Memories from the bombing haunt Seiji and Michi. Describe some of these haunting images. How do these terrible recollections fit into the larger scope of the book?

6. Tradition and heritage are major themes throughout this novel. How are they treated differently by Japanese and American characters? Does the cultural distinction prohibit Barbara from participating in Japanese traditions?

7. Why are Hiroshima survivors, "hibakusha," tainted? Do you think Seji is correct by saying hibakusha never love?

8. What does the plum tree symbolize?

9. Why did Michi leave Barbara her papers? Explain what it means to have "an inheritance of absence." (p. 179)

10. How does Rie explain that one's true valor rises above class? Does this idea of valor above class transcend all cultures? Is this a modern idea or can it be traced throughout history?

11. Barbara realizes that Seiji is leaving out parts of Michi's writing in his translation. What secret does Barbara uncover? In what ways are Seiji's actions the result of his cultural perspective? In what ways do they transcend cultural concerns?

12. Based on *Plum Wine*, how is wartime experience different for a female? As a reader, does this change the way you think about the events and repercussions of World War II?

13. Discuss the issues relating to motherhood in the novel.

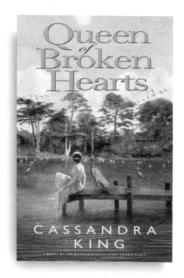

QUEEN OF BROKEN HEARTS

AUTHOR: *Cassandra King*

PUBLISHER: Hyperion, March 2007

WEBSITE: www.hyperionbooks.com
www.cassandrakingconroy.com

AVAILABLE IN:
Hardcover, 430 pages, $23.95
ISBN: (13) 978-1-4013-0177-4
ISBN: (10) 1-4013-0177-0

SUBJECT: Women's Lives/Relationships/
Personal Discovery (Fiction)

"Queen of Broken Hearts is an absolutely fabulous story of healing and hope, filled with irresistible characters that are beautifully drawn and have great insights into life. I laughed and cried, and you will, too . . . I absolutely adored this book! Congratulations, Cassandra King, on a monumental success!" —**Dorothea Benton Frank, author of** *Full of Grace*

"This novel about friendship, heartache, self-discovery and love—in all its wounding, wacky, and wonderful forms—had me laughing out loud, and then moved me to tears." —**Sandra Brown, author of** *Ricochet*

SUMMARY: It's not easy being the Queen of Broken Hearts. Just ask Clare, who has willingly assumed the mantle while her career as a divorce coach thrives. Now she's preparing to open a permanent home for the retreats she leads, on a slice of breathtaking property on the Alabama coast owned by her mother-in-law. Make that *former mother-in-law*, a colorful eccentric who teaches Clare much about love and sacrifice and living freely. When Clare's marriage ends in tragedy, her work becomes the sole focus of her life. While Clare has no problem helping the hundreds of men and women who seek her advice to mend their broken hearts, healing her own is another matter entirely. Falling in love again is the last thing she wants.

ABOUT THE AUTHOR: **Cassandra King** is the author of *Making Waves*, *The Sunday Wife*, and *The Same Sweet Girls*. A native of Alabama, she lives in South Carolina with her husband, novelist Pat Conroy.

1. In the opening scene, Clare goes to great lengths to avoid an encounter with Son Rodgers, the husband of her best friend. What is the deeper basis of their mutual dislike? Does Dory stay with her husband in spite of his flaws, or because of them? Does her devotion suggest the complicated nature of love, or simply an unhealthy relationship? Is Son's ultimate transformation plausible?

2. Two of the most important women in Clare's life are Zoe Catherine, her former mother-in-law, and Haley, her daughter, yet neither are related to her by blood. Is the author making a comment on the ties that bind us to others, and if so, do you find it true to real life?

3. On a lighter note, Clare finds herself in a love triangle with two very different men. What is it about each one that appeals to her? Which man do you find most appealing, and why? Would you have made the same choice she did?

4. Some scholars contend that myth contains the essential stories of humankind; or as Clare says to Dory, "Initiation, trial, and triumph." How does the author explain her choice of the labyrinth and Minotaur? Can you suggest other myths and how they might have been used in a different manner?

5. About the dissolution of Haley's marriage, Dory makes the following comment: "If Son dies before I do, or if we split the sheets, I won't ever marry again. Why do any of us do it?" At another point, Clare states: "I have no intention of getting involved in another relationship, not after the way my last one ended," and Lex agrees, "Going through all that crap again is the last thing I want . . ." Zoe Catherine refuses to marry her long-time lover, saying, "I get lonesome, too, but that's no reason to get married. Lonesomest folks I know are the married ones." Do you find the cynicism of these comments valid? Why, or why not?

6. Clare spends her life helping others heal and move on, yet can't do the same for herself. What is it about Mack and their relationship that she is unable to let go of?

7. The author raises disturbing questions about love and marriage, guilt and failure, fidelity and betrayal, loneliness and heartbreak. Does the final scene, with its suggestion of healing and renewal, offer any answers, or does it raise even more?

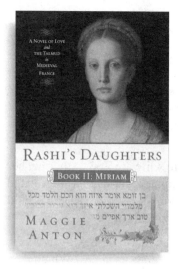

RASHI'S DAUGHTERS, BOOK II: MIRIAM

AUTHOR: *Maggie Anton*

PUBLISHER: Plume, July 2007

WEBSITE: www.penguin.com
www.rashisdaughters.com

AVAILABLE IN:
Paperback, 496 pages, $15.00
ISBN: (13) 978-0-452-28863-8
ISBN: (10) 0452288630

SUBJECT: Women's Lives/Family/
Personal Triumph (Historical Fiction)

"True to life yet colorful characters and a riveting plot, which together make for a most informative and enjoyable read. Not to be missed!"
—**Eva Etzioni-Halevy, author of *The Garden of Ruth***

"Well-researched and absolutely intriguing to read . . . what a wonderful story this is!" —**Rabbi Elliot N. Dorff, Rector and Distinguished Professor of Philosophy, American Jewish University, Los Angeles**

"Miriam gives us a fascinating glimpse into the world of Jewish women long ago. A wonderful read!" —**Rabbi Elyse Goldstein, author of *ReVisions: Seeing Torah Through a Feminist Lens***

SUMMARY: In the latter half of the eleventh century, the renowned scholar Salomon ben Isaac (or Rashi) breaks with tradition by teaching each of his three daughters, Joheved, Miriam, and Rachel, the intricacies of the Talmud. This second installment of the *Rashi's Daughters* series raises intriguing questions about women, sexuality, and tradition, while presenting a vivid picture of medieval France, and giving us insight into the timeless nature of loss, and of love.

ABOUT THE AUTHOR: **Maggie Anton** lives with her husband in Glendale, California. *Rashi's Daughters, Book I, Joheved* was her first novel. She is working on *Rashi's Daughters, Book III: Rachel*, as well as a translation of *Machzor Vitry*.

Conversation Starters for *Rashi's Daughters, Book I: Joheved*
are available on *Reading Group Choices*' website.

1. The prologue explains the social, political, and financial status of Jewish men and women in eleventh-century Europe. Also, it summarizes events that we might have read about, in detail, in *Rashi's Daughters, Book I: Joheved.* For those who haven't yet read *Book I:* Was this prologue enough? Did you find it difficult, or relatively easy, to jump right into Miriam's story? (For those who have read *Book I:* Did you find any of *Book II* helpful in refreshing your memory?)

2. Similarly, there a glossary of terms at the end of her novel. Was it essential to your comprehension and enjoyment of the novel?

3. Discuss Miriam's multiple roles as midwife, mohelet, mother, and spouse, and Judah's conflict between his homosexual feelings and his religious fervor. How can we, in the twenty-first century, relate to their predicaments?

4. What is Anton saying about the nature of loss, based on the different ways she presents it in this novel? Develop a statement of theme by drawing on specific examples from the book.

5. Miriam's marriage to Judah is one of compromise, but—as she observes at the end of the novel—out of her sisters, she is the only woman who is able to live in the same house as her husband throughout the year. In what additional ways is her marriage to Judah positive, if not ideal?

6. What does the book tell us about fate? In particular, does fate have anything to do with love?

7. Compare the eleventh-century attitude toward homosexual desire to that in the twenty-first century.

8. Discuss the Notzrim, or Christian, characters in contrast to the Jewish characters in the book. Do they help us understand the relationship between the Christian and Jewish communities in mid-eleventh-century Europe? How do their relationships help put history into perspective for us?

9. Discuss, too, the ways that the three sisters represent different female archetypes, in terms of physical appearance and in terms of character and spirit. Also, do you find any other uses of symbolism in the book?

10. Miriam appears to be the sister least ruled by her emotions, and yet, ironically enough, the most empathetic. Discuss the contradictory parts of Miriam's nature, and how they combine to make her an interesting, vivid, and realistic heroine.

11. Finally, how does this book compare with other historical fiction you may have read? What makes it unique, and what have you learned from it?

THE RED TENT
10th Anniversary Edition

AUTHOR: *Anita Diamant*

PUBLISHER: Picador USA, August 2007

WEBSITE: www.picadorusa.com
www.anitadiamant.com

AVAILABLE IN:
Paperback, 352 pages, $15.00
ISBN: (13) 978-0-312-42729-0
ISBN: (10) 0-312-42729-8

SUBJECT: Women's Lives/Family/
History (Fiction)

"By giving a voice to Dinah, one of the silent female characters in Genesis, the novel has struck a chord with women who may have felt left out of biblical history. It celebrates mothers and daughters and the mysteries of the life cycle." —**Los Angeles Times**

"An intense, vivid novel. . . . It is tempting to say that The Red Tent *is what the Bible would be like if it had been written by women, but only Diamant could have given it such sweep and grace."* —**The Boston Globe**

SUMMARY: A decade after the publication of this hugely popular international bestseller, Picador releases the tenth anniversary edition of *The Red Tent.*

Told in Dinah's voice, this novel reveals the traditions and turmoils of ancient womanhood—the world of the red tent. It begins with the story of her mothers—Leah, Rachel, Zilpah, and Bilhah—the four wives of Jacob. They love Dinah and give her gifts that sustain her through a hard-working youth, a calling to midwifery, and a new home in a foreign land. Dinah's story reaches out from a remarkable period of early history, and creates an intimate connection with the past.

ABOUT THE AUTHOR: **Anita Diamant** is an award-winning journalist and author of five books about contemporary Jewish life, including *The New Jewish Wedding* and *Choosing a Jewish Life.* Her works of fiction include *Good Harbor* and *The Last Days of Dogtown.* She lives in Massachusetts.

1. Read Genesis 34 and discuss how *The Red Tent* changes your perspective on Dinah's story and also on the story of Joseph that follows. Does *The Red Tent* raise questions about other women in the Bible? Does it make you want to re-read the Bible and imagine other untold stories that lay hidden between the lines?

2. Discuss the marital dynamics of Jacob's family. He has four wives; compare his relationship with each woman.

3. What do you make of the relationships among the four wives?

4. Dinah is rich in "mothers." Discuss the differences or similarities in her relationship with each woman.

5. Childbearing and childbirth are central to *The Red Tent*. How do the fertility childbearing and birthing practices differ from contemporary life? How are they similar? How do they compare with your own experiences as a mother or father?

6. Discuss Jacob's role as a father. Does he treat Dinah differently from his sons? Does he feel differently about her? If so, how?

7. Discuss Dinah's twelve brothers. Discuss their relationships with each other, with Dinah, and with Jacob and his four wives. Are they a close family?

8. Female relationships figure largely in *The Red Tent*. Discuss the importance of Inna, Tabea, Werenro, and Meryt.

9. In the novel, Rebecca is presented as an Oracle. Goddesses are venerated along with gods. What do you think of this culture, in which the Feminine has not yet been totally divorced from the Divine? How does El, the God of Abraham, Isaac, and Jacob, fit into this?

10. Dinah's point of view is often one of an outsider, an observer. What effect does this have on the narrative? What effect does this have on the reader?

11. The book travels from Haran (contemporary Iraq/Syria), through Canaan and into Shechem (Israel), and into Egypt. What strikes you about the cultural differences Dinah encounters vis-à-vis food, clothing, work, and male-female relationships?

12. In *The Red Tent*, we see Dinah grow from childhood to old age. Discuss how she changes and matures. What lessons does she learn from life? If you had to pick a single word to describe the sum of her life, what word would you choose? How would Dinah describe her own life experience?

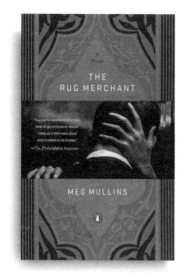

THE RUG MERCHANT

AUTHOR: *Meg Mullins*

PUBLISHER: Penguin Books, June 2007

WEBSITE: us.penguingroup.com
    www.megmullins.com

AVAILABLE IN:
Paperback, 272 pages, $14.00
ISBN: (13) 978-0-14-311209-9
ISBN: (10) 0-1311209-0

SUBJECT: Relationships/Cultural Issues/Personal Discovery (Fiction)

"Quiet and unassuming, this debut is as rich as the hand-woven rugs Ushman sells, with colorful descriptions and complex characters that provide a rewarding study in contrasts between the joy of love and the pain of vulnerability." —**Library Journal**

"A powerful experience that does what all good literature should: it tells us a little more about what it means to be human." —**The Philadelphia Inquirer**

SUMMARY: At the heart of Meg Mullins's debut novel is one of the most touchingly believable characters in recent fiction, a gentle soul in the body of an Iranian exile in New York. Ushman Khan sells exquisite hand-woven rugs to a wealthy clientele that he treats with perfect rectitude. He is lonely, and his loneliness becomes unbearable when he learns that his wife in Iran is leaving him. But when a young woman named Stella comes into his store, what ensues is a love story that is all the more moving because its protagonists understand tragedy. *The Rug Merchant* will sweep readers away with its inspiring, character-rich tale about shaking free from disappointment and finding connection and acceptance in whatever form they appear.

ABOUT THE AUTHOR: **Meg Mullins** attended Barnard College and earned her MFA from Columbia University. Her short stories have appeared in numerous publications including *The Sonoran Review, The Baltimore Review, The Iowa Review* and *TriQuarterly*. The story that formed the basis of this novel appeared in *The Best American Short Stories 2002*. She lives in New Mexico with her husband and their two children.

1. If Ushman had not "stolen" the rug, would anything really have turned out differently? Later, he throws out the rug. Why?

2. Our three principal characters all seem to be in search of something. What does each character in the novel gain/learn from the other?

3. Is Stella truly devastated by Ushman's relationship with Mrs. Roberts, or is she subconsciously looking for a way out of her relationship with Ushman, as he suspects? Why might she wish the relationship to end?

4. When Ushman tells Mrs. Roberts that her coveted carpet is no longer available, she seems oddly pleased, and "it makes Ushman angry, that to want something she can't have is an indulgence." In the next moments, Ushman lies down and Mrs. Roberts lies down next to him, silently and without touching him, "as a wife would." Why does the author include this moment? How might it foreshadow later events?

5. Discuss the significance of Mrs. Roberts's asking Ushman to pray in front of her, and what the various carpets represent throughout the novel.

6. Ushman is thrilled when Stella comes to visit him for the first time. Seeing her distress, he invites her to rest in his store and she sleeps for several hours. When she wakes up, Ushman suddenly feels angry at himself and begins to escort her out, but then seems to change his mind (p. 87). Why does he change his mind? Why does he choose this moment to blurt out that he wishes his mother would die?

7. After first wishing harm to Farak's baby, Ushman now feels anguish and sympathy toward her after learning she is "marked" by a purple blotch across her temple: "Only now that he has something to cherish does he want the universe to be forgiving" (p. 185), he thinks to himself, upon reflecting what he has gained from his relationship with Stella. But just a few pages later he tells the Vietnamese prostitute, "Your sad story does not concern me." She, like Ushman, is also an outsider, so why does his newfound compassion not spill over to her? Why did he ever allow himself to be with this prostitute in the first place?

8. *The Rug Merchant* is, at its essence, the story of a romance between two very different people. Can you think of other examples in literature of unlikely couples or cross-cultural relationships? How do these usually work out in the end?

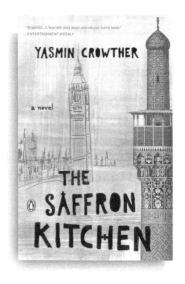

THE SAFFRON KITCHEN

AUTHOR: *Yasmin Crowther*

PUBLISHER: Penguin Books
September 2007

WEBSITE: www.penguin.com

AVAILABLE IN:
Paperback, 272 pages, $14.00
ISBN: 978-0-14-311274-7

SUBJECT: Culture & World Issues,
Identity (Fiction)

"The Saffron Kitchen *marks Yasmin Crowther out as a novelist of exceptional honesty and grace.*" —*Daily Telegraph,* **London**

"*Absorbing family drama . . . an unusual and satisfying read.*"
—*The Guardian,* **London**

SUMMARY: In what is certain to be one of the most talked-about fiction debuts of the year, Yasmin Crowther paints a magnificent portrait of betrayal and retribution set against a backdrop of Iran's tumultuous history, dramatic landscapes, and cultural beauty. The story begins on a blustery day in London, when Maryam Mazar's dark secrets and troubled past surface violently with tragic consequences for her pregnant daughter, Sara. Burdened by guilt, Maryam leaves her comfortable English home for the remote village in Iran where she was raised and disowned by her father. When Sara decides to follow her, she learns the price that her mother had to pay for her freedom and of the love she left behind.

ABOUT THE AUTHOR: **Yasmin Crowther** lives in London. She grew up in an Anglo-Iranian household. This is her first novel.

1. The Middle East is very much in the news these days, and perhaps never before has it been more on the mind of Westerners. What issues did *The Saffron Kitchen* bring up for you, and did it change or influence your idea of Iran in any way?

2. Maryam says she hits Saeed to make him strong, just as her own father hit her as a girl. Do you believe this? Why or why not? Discuss the reasons you think Maryam feels so angry at Saeed. What does he represent to her? Why do you think some abused people grow up to continue that abuse, while others vow never to repeat the "sins of their fathers"?

3. When Maryam returns home after taking Sara to the hospital, she says to herself, "I should never have left." What is she referring to? The hospital? Iran? And what does she mean by this? How does her statement foreshadow what happens in the rest of the novel?

4. What is the moral of the Gossemarbart story and how does it relate to Maryam's own story? Discuss the symbolism of the stone woman and its significance in the novel.

5. Sara and Saeed form a strong connection with one another. Talk about the things they have in common, the things that make them different, and how they might derive comfort from one another.

6. Farnoosh, Hassan's unmarried daughter, says to Maryam, "You think [having your family is] enough? When you leave yours behind? Please don't patronize me." Can you explain Farnoosh's point of view? Do you see Maryam as selfish? Why or why not?

7. "For each freedom we choose, we must give up another," Maryam says. What does she mean in terms of her own life? Do you agree or disagree, and why?

8. What do you think Maryam wants for Sara? Does Sara have a right to be angry at her mother? How would you feel, as a daughter or son, if your mother left you to return to the place of her birth?

9. Where does Maryam's love for Iran end and her love for Ali begin? Are they separate?

10. Discuss how the author uses the color saffron as a symbol throughout the novel. What does it represent, to Maryam, to Sara, to Saeed?

11. Think about the different worlds to which you belong. Consider the transitions between these worlds and discuss how navigating these transitions affects your life.

SAVE YOUR OWN

AUTHOR: *Elisabeth Brink*

PUBLISHER: Mariner, June 2007

WEBSITE: www.marinerbooks.com
www.elisabethbrink.com

AVAILABLE IN:
Paperback, 288 pages, $13.95
ISBN: (13) 978-0-618-87193-3
ISBN: (10) 0-618-87193-4

SUBJECT: Women's Lives/Personal
Discovery/Relationships (Fiction)

A Book Sense Notable Book

"[Elisabeth Brink is] *clearly a gifted writer with a slant of mind, sense of humor, and turn of phrase all her own.*" —*Seattle Times*

"*Gillian Cormier-Brandenburg is one of the most original characters I've encountered in recent fiction, a winning mix of intellect, innocence, and anxiety. I fell in love with her, and I think you will, too.*" —**Stephen McCauley, author of *Alternatives to Sex* and *The Object of My Affection***

SUMMARY: Gillian Cormier-Brandenburg is a virginal, narcoleptic, atheistic Harvard Divinity School student about to complete her Ph.D. When the faculty deems her dissertation unsuitable and threatens to revoke her fellowship funding, Gillian—determined to defend her topic—sets out to gather research. She takes a job at a halfway house for recovering addicts and struggles to become an unlikely figure of authority. The women at Responsibility House challenge Gillian at every step, and eventually inspire her to confront her limitations and find her place in the world.

ABOUT THE AUTHOR: **Elisabeth Brink** grew up in Boston, graduated from Brown University and earned a Ph.D. in American literature from Brandeis University, and lived for six years in the rural Midwest, where she was an editor at a children's magazine. She has taught writing and literature at Harvard, Tufts, and Boston College. Her fiction has garnered her fellowships in Prague and St. Petersburg, and her stories were nominated for a Pushcart Prize by the late Andre Dubus. *Save Your Own* is her first novel. She lives in Newburyport, Massachusetts.

1. Do you consider Gillian a strong character? How would you define strength?

2. Some of the characters in the book are former criminals and drug addicts. How—if at all—do you think this might have affected the way you viewed them as you were reading the book?

3. Which characters did you sympathize with most? Which characters did you find the least sympathetic? How did your sympathies shift over the course of the novel?

4. Discuss the role humor plays throughout the story. How does comedy contribute to the way we experience the book?

5. Much of the conflict at Responsibility House occurs between Stacy, a rigid rule follower, and the rebellious Janet. Which character is more responsible? More admirable?

6. At first Gillian struggles to enforce the Responsibility House's Handbook of Policies and Procedures, but as time goes on she begins to question them. What leads to this change in her understanding?

7. Why is it important to Gillian to write the Pink Book, which reduces the number of rules to two? Do you see the Pink Book as an improvement over the Handbook of Policies and Procedures? Why or why not? What are the dangers inherent in each?

8. Why does Gillian refuse to change her thesis topic of "secular conversion experiences"? What does this say about her character and actions?

9. Is there such a thing as a "secular conversion experience"? What are some examples of those experiences in the book? What are some of the ways "conversion" can take place? Do you think Gillian capable of having a conversion experience? What else might it be called?

10. Why do you think the author included an epilogue? Does your perception of Gillian change after reading it? How? Discuss how her earlier experiences may have helped shape the rest of her life.

11. What do you think the title, *Save Your Own*, means?

SAVING GRACES
Finding Solace and Strength from Friends and Strangers

AUTHOR: *Elizabeth Edwards*

PUBLISHER: Broadway Books, August 2007

WEBSITE: www.elizabethedwardsbook.com
www.randomhouse.com/broadway

AVAILABLE IN:
Paperback, 384 pages, $14.95
ISBN: 978-0-7679-2538-9

SUBJECT: Biography/Inspiration/Personal Challenges (Memoir)

*"Edwards's memoir is not about cancer, politics or even unbearable loss (though the description of her grief is heart-wrenching). It's about the value of people coming together to support each other. You'll find no celebrity gossip here. But like the kiss on the forehead her husband gave her at the end of their first date, this memoir is disarmingly moving."—**Publishers Weekly***

SUMMARY: Elizabeth Edwards charmed and inspired America with her smart, likable, courageous, down-to-earth personality as she campaigned for her husband, then vice-presidential candidate John Edwards. Now she shares her experiences in *Saving Graces*, an incandescent memoir of Edwards' trials, tragedies, and triumphs, and of how various communities celebrated her joys and lent her steady strength and quiet hope in darker times.

ABOUT THE AUTHOR: **Elizabeth Edwards,** a lawyer, has worked for the North Carolina Attorney General's office and at the law firm Merriman, Nichols, and Crampton in Raleigh, and she has also taught legal writing as an adjunct instructor at the law school of North Carolina University. She lives in Chapel Hill, North Carolina.

1. Throughout *Saving Graces*, Elizabeth Edwards describes her great friend, Hargrave McElroy. Who is the Hargrave in your life?

2. What aspects of Elizabeth's childhood prepared her for a high-profile future? What aspects of her youth would later challenge her understanding of the world?

3. What did Elizabeth's parents and grandparents teach her about parenting? Which of their legacies are still a part of her life?

4. Discuss the memoir's title. How do you define grace? What is Elizabeth's message about human nature in times of crisis?

5. What has kept Elizabeth's and John's marriage strong?

6. What does Elizabeth tell us about the experience of grief of losing her son, and the best ways to bring comfort to someone. If you had participated in her online group, how would you have responded to the religious debate that was sparked?

7. At Wade's funeral, his father read these lines from Wade's Outward Bound journal: "The course director said the solo is where you become a man. I disagree with that ... I think that you never really stop maturing and growing as a person." What does it mean to possess maturity? What were your equivalents of a challenging "solo"? Has your personal growth ever truly been achieved solo?

8. How have the expectations for various populations—families, politicians, military personnel, first ladies—changed since the 1950s and 1960s?

9. What are your recollections of the 2004 presidential election? What campaign details were you surprised to discover in *Saving Graces*?

10. The subtitle of *Saving Graces* reminds us of the strangers who have also helped Elizabeth and John. Who have been the least-expected strangers to help you during a crisis? What opportunities are in your life right now to be the saving grace for someone else?

11. What insight does Elizabeth's story impart about the emotional and medical aspects of a breast cancer diagnosis? What does her case indicate about current debates over whether mammograms are worthwhile?

12. Though Elizabeth's life has been marked by loss, she and John have also experienced beautiful blessings. What determines whether our losses overshadow our joys?

SPECIAL TOPICS IN CALAMITY PHYSICS

AUTHOR: **Marisha Pessl**

PUBLISHER: Penguin Books, April 2007

WEBSITE: us.penguingroup.com

AVAILABLE IN:
Paperback, 528 pages, $15.00
ISBN: (13) 978-0-14-311212-9
ISBN: (10) 0-14-311212-0

SUBJECT: Coming of Age/ Relationships/Intrigue (Fiction)

"This skylarking book will leave readers salivating for more. The joys of this shrewdly playful narrative lie not only in the high-low darts and dives of Pessl's tricky plotting, but in her prose, which floats and runs as if by instinct, unpremeditated and unerring." —**The New York Times Book Review**

"Required reading for devotees of inventive new fiction."
—**The New York Times**

"Hip, ambitious and imaginative." —**Los Angeles Times**

SUMMARY: "Dazzling," (*People*) "Exuberant," (Vogue) "marvelously entertaining," (*The Dallas Morning News*)—Marisha Pessl's mesmerizing debut has critics raving and heralds the arrival of a vibrant new voice in American fiction. At the center of this "cracking good read" is clever, deadpan Blue van Meer, who has a head full of literary, philosophical, scientific, and cinematic knowledge. But she could use some friends. Upon entering the elite St. Gallway school, she finds some—a clique of eccentrics known as the Bluebloods. One drowning and one hanging later, Blue finds herself puzzling out a byzantine murder mystery. Nabokov meets Donna Tartt (then invites the rest of the Western Canon to the party) in this novel—with "visual aids" drawn by the author—that has won over readers of all ages.

ABOUT THE AUTHOR: **Marisha Pessl** grew up in Asheville, North Carolina, and graduated Phi Beta Kappa form Columbia University. *Special Topics in Calamity Physics* is her first novel.

1. Blue describes herself as a "Jane Goodall," an observer not a main actor. What did you think of her when we first meet her? How does she change over the course of the novel? At the end, what new characteristics has she acquired?

2. How does Blue's attitude toward her father begin to change? Does he alter the way that he treats her? Try to imagine their future relationship; how might they feel toward each other?

3. Who was Hannah Schneider? What does Blue learn about her past, and about how they are linked? Do you have sympathy for Hannah? Was she well-intentioned or do you think she was disturbed and dangerous?

4. Why is Hannah so interested in Blue? How does she encourage Blue to act? Is she a good influence on Blue and the others?

5. Small-town America is also a subject of this book; Gareth is a "perennial visiting lecturer," who raises Blue in a series of obscure towns throughout America. Think back to some of the places that they have lived, and the accompanying Americana. How would you describe this America? How is it different from other, more mainstream, depictions of the country? Do you recognize these places? What do you think Blue thinks of them?

6. What does Zach offer that the others cannot? What do you think he sees in Blue? Why do you think the Bluebloods are so disparaging toward him? What role does he play in Blue's transformation?

7. What is Blue's relationship to some of her father's "June Bugs" (girlfriends)? Does she grow more sympathetic to them? Consider some of the specific encounters Blue has with women Gareth is involved with. What does the incident with "Kitty," in particular, teach her?

8. The relationship between ideology and violence is a subtext that turns into a main theme. Who is particularly ideological or political in this book? What do they believe in and advocate for? Try to trace Gareth van Meer's beliefs, in particular, by returning to earlier passages in the novel where Blue mentions his ideas, reading material, or lectures.

9. At the end of the book, Blue is faced with a hard choice about the information she has uncovered. How does she act and why? Though he never says, do you think her father is proud of her ultimate decision about the secret she uncovers? What does her decision, which costs her plenty, tell you about Blue's morals and inner strength? What would you have done?

STILL LIFE WITH CHICKENS
Starting Over in a House by the Sea

AUTHOR: *Catherine Goldhammer*

PUBLISHER: Plume, April 2007

WEBSITE: www.penguin.com
www.catherinegoldhammer.com

AVAILABLE IN:
Paperback, 192 pages, $12.00
ISBN: (13) 978-0-452-28848-5
ISBN: (10) 0452288487

SUBJECT: Family/Women's Lives/
Personal Discovery (Memoir)

"Still Life with Chickens *teaches the art of moving on . . . and reminds the reader that—through friends, family, inspiration, humor, and a little chutzpah—anything is possible."* —**Ann Hood, author of** *Somewhere Off the Coast of Maine*

"*Told in wry and poignant prose,* Still Life with Chickens *offers a testament to new beginnings."* —**Joan Anderson, author of the national bestseller** *A Year By the Sea*

SUMMARY: Catherine Goldhammer wakes in middle age to find herself newly separated and several tax brackets poorer, forced by circumstance to move from the affluent New England suburb into a new, more rustic life by the sea. Against all logic, partly to please her daughter and partly for reasons not clear to her at the time, she begins this year of transition by purchasing six baby chickens—whose job, she comes to suspect, is to pull her and her daughter forward, out of one life and into another.

Still Life with Chickens is an unforgettable lesson in hope, in starting over, and in the transcendent wisdom that can often be found in the most unlikely of places.

ABOUT THE AUTHOR: **Catherine Goldhammer**'s poetry has been published in the *Georgia Review* and the *Ohio Review*, and by *Innerer Klang Press*. She lives in a small cottage on the coast of New England with her daughter, her dog, a cat named Monkey, and a small flock of chickens.

1. What do the chickens represent to her and why are they essential to her new life?

2. Discuss the differences between the town the author calls Hearts-are-Cold and the neighborhood she moves to. Why do you think she is more comfortable in her new surroundings? What about the new neighborhood appeals to her? Why?

3. Discuss how the author's daughter changes and grows during this transition in their lives. How does she influence her mother? Why is she a source of such awe? Who in your own life plays that role?

4. Of all the houses the author sees, why do you think she chooses the one she does? What is she looking for? What does she find?

5. Discuss the following passage: "The logistics of moving, the yard, the legal documents, Penny and her perfume, these were temporary. The chickens were the thread, the real thing that pulled us, stumbling and fearful into the future" (54).

6. What is the role of the "Moon Women"? How do they contribute to the author's ability to move on with her life?

7. When the author and her daughter are established in their new home, the author writes, "So what was is about chickens that made me want to set up my lawn chair out there by the chicken yard, sit down with a glass of lemonade, and watch? They are simple" (168). Why is the simplicity of the chickens so attractive? Do you think the chickens are simple? In what ways are they simple and in what ways are they difficult for the author and her daughter?

8. Throughout the memoir, the author remarks numerous times that her house was made possible because others were kind to her. What are some examples of the kindness in the people she met throughout the process? How did they help her? What roles did they play in building the house and helping her start her life over?

9. In what ways does the author change during the renovation process? What literal and emotional changes occur? Do you feel that she has grown and changed by the end of the memoir? How?

10. Discuss the Alice's Adventures in Wonderland quote at the beginning of the book. Why did the author choose it? How does it relate to her own story? Do you think that she has accomplished impossible things?

SWEETNESS IN THE BELLY

AUTHOR: *Camilla Gibb*

PUBLISHER: Penguin Books, April 2007

WEBSITE: www.penguin.com

AVAILABLE IN:
Paperback, 368 pages, $14.00
ISBN: (13) 978-0-143-03872-6
ISBN: (10) 0-14-303872-9

SUBJECT: Culture & World Issues/
Personal Challenges/Women's Lives
(Fiction)

"Gibb's territory is urgently modern and controversial, but she enters it softly, with grace, integrity and a lovely compassionate story. A poem to belief and to the displaced—humane, resonant, original, impressive."
—**Kirkus Reviews** (starred review)

SUMMARY: When Lilly is eight years old, her pot-smoking hippy British parents leave her at a Sufi shrine in Morocco and inform her they will be back to collect her in three days. Three weeks later, she learns they've been murdered. Lilly fills that hollow in her life with the intense study and memorization of the Qur'an. In Harar, even her very traditional Muslim headscarves cannot hide her white skin in her new and strange surroundings. She eventually builds a life for herself teaching children the Qur'an, and she finds herself falling in love with an idealistic young doctor. But the two are wrenched apart when Lilly is again forced to flee, for her safety and his, this time to London. Despite her British roots, Lilly discovers she is as much of an outsider in London as a Muslim as she was in Harar as a white foreigner.

ABOUT THE AUTHOR: **Camilla Gibb** was born in London, England, and grew up in Toronto. Her two previous novels, *Mouthing the Words*, winner of the City of Toronto Book Award in 2000, and *The Petty Details of So-And-So's Life* have been published in 18 countries and translated into 14 languages. She is one of 21 writers on the "Orange Futures List"—a list of young writers to watch. Camilla lives in Toronto, where she is writer-in-residence at the University of Toronto.

1. Discuss Lilly's role as an outsider and her struggle for acceptance both as a *farenji* in Harar and as a white Muslim in London. Who else in the novel could be considered an outsider?

2. What do the words "family" and "home" mean to Lilly? How does her view of herself as an orphan evolve over the course of the novel?

3. "Faith has accompanied me over time and geography and upheaval," says Lilly. For her, love and Islam "have always been one." Did *Sweetness in the Belly* in any way alter or broaden your understanding of Islam? Consider, for instance, the notion of jihad or holy war.

4. *Sweetness in the Belly* alternates between Harar, Ethiopia, in the 1970s, and London, England, in the 1980s and early 1990s. What qualities does this crosscutting of time and place impart to the narrative?

5. In the chapter entitled "Exile," Lilly observes that "the smell of coffee draws women together, an olfactory call throughout a neighborhood luring women from their homes to gather . . ." Later in the chapter, the act of twisting a mortar over coffee beans and cardamom triggers in her a surge of nightmarish images from the Red Terror. Of the many lush sensory details in the novel—both fair and foul—which affected you the most?

6. While living in Ethiopia, Camilla Gibb witnessed a female circumcision. A doctoral student in social anthropology at the time, she says she had to "understand it in the context of the community in which it was taking place, and not judge." When Nouria's daughters are circumcised in *Sweetness in the Belly*, how does Lilly react as the only Western-born character in the scene? How did you react as a reader?

7. Based on your reading of *Sweetness in the Belly*, what feelings and psychological states are associated with the experience of exile? How do Amina and Yusuf, for example, cope with their respective traumas?

8. In Harar, Aziz is called a "black savage, African slave, barbarian, pagan." In London, Lilly is called a "white fu'in Paki." Discuss the notion of "otherness" in the novel. How do artificial divisions manifest themselves based on ethnicity, class, race, religion, and gender?

9. Discuss the ways in which the female characters ensure their survival and empower themselves despite the gender divisions within their communities.

10. What does Lilly mean when she says that Aziz "unveiled" her? How does she reconcile her love for him with her love of Islam?

THEY DID IT WITH LOVE

AUTHOR: *Kate Morgenroth*

PUBLISHER: Plume, December 2007

WEBSITE: www.penguin.com
www.katemorgenroth.com

AVAILABLE IN:
Paperback, 336 pages, $14.00
ISBN: (13) 978-0-452-28897-3
ISBN: (10) 0-452-28897-5

SUBJECT: Intrigue/Relationships/
Women's Lives (Fiction)

"Compulsively readable. Filled with wonderfully wicked characters and brilliant twists and turns." —**Lisa Lutz, author of** *The Spellman Files*

"I thoroughly enjoyed They Did It with Love. *It was a deliciously entertaining romp through the thickets of suburban marriage and murder."*
—**Carol Goodman,** *The New York Times* **bestselling author of** *The Lake of Dead Languages*

SUMMARY: Sofie and her husband have decided to trade their Manhattan apartment for a house in Greenwich, Connecticut. But the oak-shaded streets are not the tranquil retreat that Sofie expected. When Julia, a member of Sofie's new neighborhood book club, turns up dead, things get messy. Sofie discovers that everybody has something to hide, including her own husband.

As Sofie wades through a swamp of suburban secrets, it becomes clear that no one's life is exactly what it seems to be. The investigation into the mysterious circumstances surrounding Julia's death uncovers the lies behind the façade. *They Did It with Love* is a delightful, twisty, and twisted exploration of the things we'll do for love.

ABOUT THE AUTHOR: **Kate Morgenroth** is the author of *Kill Me First* and *Saved*, and two YA novels, *Jude* and *Echo*. She lives in New York.

1. Did you figure out who the murderer was before the reveal?

2. How did you feel when you discovered who killed Julia? Did you feel sympathetic to the murderer?

3. What clues does Morgenroth give to the murderer's identity throughout the novel? Are there false clues that point to others?

4. There are several different marriages and serious relationships portrayed in the novel. Which ones do you think will survive for the long haul and why do you think those characters work as a couple?

5. Would you join Priscilla's book group if you were invited?

6. Priscilla has very specific rules for her book group. Do you agree with her rules or disagree with them? How important are rules in your book group (supposing you are in one)?

7. Would you characterize your neighborhood as a close community? Is your community like the one that Morgenroth portrays here, with competition over holiday decoration and parties and secrets from your neighbors?

8. Do you think that a community in the suburbs is more prone to secrets and competitive nature than a community in a city? Why or why not?

9. Did you relate to Sophie's fears and concerns about moving out of the city to a suburban environment? Have you made a similar move and were you glad you did?

10. If you are living in a small town or a suburb now, could you imagine yourself living in a large city?

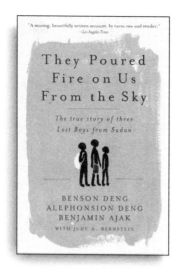

THEY POURED FIRE ON US FROM THE SKY

The True Story of Three Lost Boys from Sudan

AUTHORS: *Alephonsion Deng, Benson Deng,* **and** *Benjamin Ajak, with Judy A. Bernstein*

PUBLISHER: PublicAffairs, June 2006

WEBSITE: www.publicaffairsbooks.com

AVAILABLE IN:
Paperback, 311 pages, $12.95
ISBN: (13) 978-1-58648-388-3
ISBN: (10) 1-58648-388-9

SUBJECT: History/Cultural & World Issues/Personal Triumph (Memoir)

"[T]ender and lyrical . . . one of the most riveting stories ever told of African childhoods—and a stirring tale of courage. . . . Anyone interested in Africa, its children or the human will to survive should read this book. This beautifully told volume . . . will remain on my desk for years to come." —**Emily Wax,** *Washington Post*

SUMMARY: Across Sudan, between 1987 and 1989, tens of thousands of young boys took flight from the massacres of Sudan's civil war in search of refuge. They became known as the Lost Boys. They walked nearly one thousand miles, first to Ethiopia and then, driven back into Sudan, toward Kenya, sustained only by the sheer will to live. *They Poured Fire on Us from the Sky* is three boys' account of that unimaginable journey—a captivating portrait of a childhood lost to war, and of the perseverance of the human spirit.

ABOUT THE AUTHORS: **Alephonsion Deng**, **Benson Deng**, and **Benjamin Ajak** relocated to the United States in 2001, through the efforts of the International Rescue Committee. Now in their mid-twenties, they are pursuing college education and careers and speak frequently throughout the country on behalf of the Lost Boys. **Judy A. Bernstein** is a volunteer mentor of the San Diego International Rescue Committee and co-founder of the IRC Lost Boys Education Fund.

1. What do Judy Bernstein and her son find most striking about Benson, Alepho, and Benjamin when they arrive in San Diego? What would be your own reaction if you were meeting the boys during their first few days in America? Would you find it frustrating? Exciting? What advice would you give the boys' for adapting to American society?

2. What did you find most troubling about the boys' experiences? Which moments struck you as particularly emotionally moving? Why?

3. How do the voices of Benson, Alepho, and Benjamin differ? How are they similar? Do they have distinguishing characteristics? Was there a writer who you felt most connected to?

4. Benson asserts that hunger "makes you like a wild animal." While enduring years of starvation, how do the boys maintain their humanity? If you were involved in a similarly desperate situation, what would you do to preserve your compassion?

5. Why was education so important to the boys—especially to Benson? How does the boys' desire to learn compare to young people in America who you know?

6. Benson and Alepho have heard some outlandish rumors about America. What were they, and what perhaps inspired their formation? Are there countries or cultures that we make similarly misinformed judgments about today?

7. What are the boys' attitudes toward women? Compare their perceptions of African women to our perceptions of American women.

8. During their journeys, Benson, Alepho, and Benjamin each meet many people—some fellow refugees and some not. Which of these secondary characters have the most influence on the writers' stories? Which leave the strongest impressions on you?

9. How do you think the boys' age and lack of guardians affected their travels? Was it always to their detriment? How might their experiences have been different had the boys been older?

10. How do the refugees help each other despite living in confining environments of absolute poverty? How do they manage to assert some control over their own lives?

11. Why do you think there so few "Lost Girls"?

12. The efforts of aid groups like the UN are sometimes a mixed blessing to the refugees. Why is this? What do you think could be done so that their influence would be wholly helpful?

THIS IS NOT THE LIFE I ORDERED

50 Ways to Keep Your Head Above Water When Life Keeps Dragging You Down

AUTHORS: *Deborah Collins Stephens, Michealene Cristini Risley, Jackie Speier, and Jan Yanehiro*

PUBLISHER: Conari Press, March 2007

WEBSITE: www.conari.com
www.thisisnotthelifeiordered.com

AVAILABLE IN:
Hardcover, 224 pages, $19.95
ISBN: 978-1-57324-305-6

SUBJECT: Personal Challenges/
Personal Triumph/Inspiration (Nonfiction)

"This book is the needed inspiration to survive the worst luck and circumstances that catch women unexpectedly." —**Amy Tan, best-selling author of** ***The Joy Luck Club***

"I wish I had this book thirty years ago. What a welcome source of inspiration and insight." —**Linda Ellerbee, journalist, award-winning television producer, best-selling author, breast cancer survivor, and mom**

SUMMARY: They were four women whom destiny threw together over a decade ago. Collectively, they experienced the extreme joys and deep sorrows that life offers up. The authors have a history of six marriages, ten children, four stepchildren, six dogs, two miscarriages, two cats, a failed adoption, widowhood, and foster parenthood. They have built companies, lost companies, and sold companies. Meeting monthly for over a decade, they shared their lives with one another and encouraged one another. The remarkable results are this collection of lessons and stories and wisdom.

ABOUT THE AUTHORS: **Deborah Collins Stephens** is the cofounder and managing partner of the Center for Innovative Leadership and the author of six books, three of which have been best-sellers: *Maslow on Management, One Size Fits One*, and *Revisiting the Human Side of Enterprise.* **Jackie Speiers** has devoted her life to public service, most recently as a California State Senator. **Jan Yanehiro** is a ground-breaking, Emmy-winning journalist. **Michealene Cristini Risley** is an entrepreneur and documentary filmmaker.

1. The book opens with the personal stories of each of the authors who were juggling only slightly less-than worst-case scenario events. Do they all feel like the female version of the book of Job? Or, are they pretty normal women going through pretty normal circumstances?

2. If you were Jackie Speier, would you have devoted your life to public service after being shot five times and left for dead on a tarmac in South America at the start of your career?

3. How about Michealene Cristini Risley confronting her father about a dirty family secret on his death bed? Would you have had the courage to face demons similar to those she faced?

4. After 10 years of living with a husband who was to have perished long ago from a rare lung disease, what has helped Deborah Collins Stephens to persevere?

5. How did Jan Yanehiro come back from widowhood and near bankruptcy to win a series of Emmys for her work?

6. How have these women and others in the book taught you to make courage an everyday companion?

7. If a change has happened unexpectedly in your life—loss of a job, loss of a loved one—and you've had to face questions from co-workers, friends and others, like "well, what are you going to do now?" what are some of the more creative answers you've used to deal with these dreaded questions?

8. Have there been times when you have felt you simply could not do it all, but were ashamed to ask for help? What would you do differently next time?

9. Can you identify the energy vampires in your life who leave you feeling mentally and physically exhausted after you've spent time with them? Discuss ways of either ditching or dealing with these "takers."

10. If you were to create a "to don't list" what 10 items would be on your list?

11. On the opposite spectrum from energy vampires is "dream catchers." Can you identify the dream catchers in your life? Deborah's was the blue-haired lady.

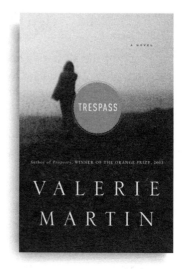

TRESPASS

AUTHOR: *Valerie Martin*

PUBLISHER: Nan A. Talese,
September 2007

WEBSITE: www.nanatalese.com

AVAILABLE IN:
Hardcover, 304 pages, $25.00
ISBN: (13) 978-0-385-51545-0
ISBN: (10) 0-385-51545-6

SUBJECT: Family/Culture & World
Issues/Relationships (Fiction)

PRAISE FOR VALERIE MARTIN:

*"An enrapturing and ruthless storyteller, Valerie Martin possesses a predator's ability to mesmerize her prey." —**Chicago Tribune***

*"The cool assurance of Martin's voice, and her capacity to say surprising things about ordinary feelings—envy, rage, and despair figure prominently—make the collection a triumph." —**The New Yorker***

SUMMARY: Chloe Dale's life is in good order. Her only child, Toby, has started his junior year at New York University; her husband is working at home on his book about the Crusades; and Chloe is creating illustrations for a special edition of *Wuthering Heights*. Yet Chloe is disturbed—by her government's foreign policy, by the poacher who roams the land behind her studio, and finally, by Toby's new girlfriend, a Croatian refugee named Salome Drago.

As Toby's obsession with Salome grows, Chloe's mistrust deepens, alienating her from her tolerant husband and besotted son. Rich with menace, the novel unfolds in a world where darkness intrudes into bright and pleasant places, a world with betrayal at its heart. In shimmering prose Valerie Martin raises the question: who shall inherit America?

ABOUT THE AUTHOR: **Valerie Martin** is the author of three collections of short fiction, most recently *The Unfinished Novel and Other Stories*, and seven novels, including *Italian Fever*, *The Great Divorce*, *Mary Reilly*, which was filmed with Julia Roberts and John Malkovich, and the 2003 Orange Prize-winning *Property*. She is also the author of a non-fiction work about St. Francis of Assisi: *Salvation: Scenes from the Life of St. Francis*. She resides in upstate New York.

1. What is Chloe's initial impression of Salome? What about her does she find so threatening? Are these the same traits that make her attractive to Toby (and, incidentally, to Brendan)? Are Chloe's perceptions accurate?

2. What are the possible reasons for Salome's seriousness, and in what ways might those reasons contribute to both her allure and her destructiveness?

3. Putting aside the question of whether Chloe's fears are justified, might they be self-fulfilling? Where else in the novel do people's fears and suspicions become self-fulfilling?

4. What does the presence of animals do for *Trespass*? In what ways do animals serve as stand-ins for the book's human actors, and how does the novel's changing perspective on them mirror its approach to human character?

5. What is the significance of Chloe's illustrations for *Wuthering Heights*? How do her thoughts about that novel and its characters seem to comment on people and events in her own life?

6. How does Brendan's work-in-progress on the life of Frederick II reflect or anticipate events in the novel?

7. Do you find it significant that that woodstove is one of the few things Salome seems to like about her future mother-in-law? What does Salome—who at times seems willing to wage war against the entire world in the service of her desires—actually desire?

8. Is the threat posed by a trespasser the fact that the trespasser wants what we have—our property, our game, our lovers, our children—and is prepared to do anything to possess them? Which of the novel's other characters might be described as a trespasser?

9. Consider the implication that a trespasser may be far less dangerous than someone who is defending himself from being trespassed against. Consider Andro's catastrophic reaction to the trespasses of his mother and sister. Consider that Iraq was invaded in the name of America's national security. Consider that the men who destroy Jelena and her family think of themselves as defenders of an old way of life.

10. When does it become apparent that the voice that periodically breaks into the Dale narrative is Jelena? When do we realize the identity of her interlocutor? Why might Martin have chosen to do this?

UNBOWED
A Memoir

AUTHOR: *Wangari Maathai*

PUBLISHER: Anchor Books, September 2007

WEBSITE: www.ReadingGroupCenter.com

AVAILABLE IN:
Paperback, 368 pages, $14.95
ISBN: 978-0-307-27520-2

SUBJECT: World Issues/Inspiration/
Women's Lives (Memoir)

**A "gripping"* memoir by the first African woman
and the first environmentalist to win the Nobel Peace Prize.**

*"Wangari Maathai's memoir is direct, honest, and beautifully written—
a gripping account of modern Africa's trials and triumphs, a universal
story of courage, persistence, and success against great odds in a noble
cause."* **—*President Bill Clinton**

SUMMARY: Born in Kenya, Wangari Maathai left to pursue her higher education in the United States earning her bachelor's and master's degrees.
Returning to Kenya, she became the first woman to earn a Ph.D. in East
and Central Africa and to head the department of veterinary medicine at
the University of Nairobi. In *Unbowed*, she recounts the political and personal beliefs that led her, in 1977, to establish the Green Belt Movement,
which spread from Kenya across Africa, helping to restore indigenous
forests while assisting rural women by paying them to plant trees in their
villages. Maathai's efforts helped transform Kenya's government into the
democracy in which she now serves as a member of Parliament. In 2004
she was awarded the Nobel Peace Prize in recognition of her "contribu-
tion to sustainable development, human rights, and peace."

ABOUT THE AUTHOR: **Wangari Muta Maathai** was born in Nyeri, Kenya,
in 1940. She is the founder of the Green Belt Movement, which, through
networks of rural women, has planted over forty million trees across
Kenya since 1977. In 2002, she was elected to Kenya's parliament in the
first free elections in a generation, and in 2003, she was appointed assis-
tant minister for the environment. She lives and works in Nairobi.

1. What aspects of her family life and her mother's approach to child-rearing, as described in "Beginnings," might have nurtured Wangari's strong, forthright, and optimistic character? How powerful was the effect of cultivating the soil on her imagination as a child?

2. How does Maathai react, upon arriving in America, to the presence of black Americans? What connection does she make between the legacy of slavery in America and the legacy of colonialism in Kenya? Is it surprising that, in the America of the early 1960s, she wasn't often the target of racism herself? Was there a similar color barrier in Kenya, prior to independence?

3. Facing the difficulties of department politics at the university, Maathai writes, "I found myself wanting to be more than the equal of some of the men I knew. I had higher aspirations and did not want to be compared with men of lesser ability and capacity. I wanted to be me." How did her male colleagues at the university react to her ambition and energy?

4. What is particularly African about Maathai's approach to the environment, and why does the erosion caused by increasing deforestation disturb her so much? Do you see the roots of her feeling for the environment in her childhood? What does the fig tree she loved as a child symbolize for her?

5. How does Maathai come to realize that activism must be grounded in the community, and that communication must be at a level all members of the community can understand? Why is she so effective in reaching out to poor and illiterate rural women in the tree-planting program?

6. Reflecting on her time in prison for treason, Maathai says, "As I sat in those cells, denying me the ability to control what happened seemed to me to be the greatest punishment the regime could mete out to me." Discuss the ways she responds to adversity and to the failure, at times, of her hopes. Which aspects of her character allow her to be so effective in fighting back against the corrupt government and encouraging others to insist upon their rights?

For the complete Reading Group Guide,
visit www.ReadingGroupCenter.com.

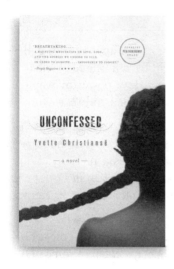

UNCONFESSED

AUTHOR: *Yvette Christiansë*

PUBLISHER: Other Press, September 2007

WEBSITE: www.otherpress.com

AVAILABLE IN:
Paperback, 360 pages, $14.95
ISBN: 978-1-59051-281-4

SUBJECT: History/Personal Challenges/
Women's Lives (Historical Fiction)

A PEN/Hemingway Award Finalist

"Impossible to put down, this work deserves a place beside such classics as Toni Morrison's Beloved *and Edward P. Jones's* The Known World.*"*
—*Library Journal* (starred review)

"A gorgeous, devastating song of freedom."
—*Kirkus Reviews* (starred review)

SUMMARY: Slavery as it existed in Africa has seldom been portrayed—and never with such texture, detail, and authentic emotion. Inspired by actual 19th-century court records, *Unconfessed* is a breathtaking literary tour de force.

A woman fit for hanging . . . condemned to death on April 30, 1823, only to have her sentence commuted to a lengthy term on the notorious Robben Island. Her fierce, sometimes tender voice recalls the dramatic events of her life—as well as its small, precious moments and pleasures.

This fiercely poetic literary debut re-creates the life of a 19th-century slave woman in a gripping tale that captures the epic sweep of history and the intimacy of daily life.

ABOUT THE AUTHOR: **Yvette Christiansë** was born in South Africa under apartheid and emigrated with her family via Swaziland to Australia at the age of eighteen. She is the author of the 1999 poetry collection *Castaway*. She lives in New York City. *Unconfessed* is her first novel.

1. Do you have any mental image of Sila? What kinds of detail emerge from her deeply introspective voice?

2. Why do you think the author chose to shift from third person to first person narrative? What does this shift achieve?

3. How and when does the tone and style of Sila's language change?

4. Can we trust Sila's account of everything? Or are there moments when we believe her and moments when we doubt her?

5. What do you think Sila keeps secret, and why?

6. What does Sila say to her friend Lys that she does not say to her son, Baro?

7. Why do you think Sila says nothing about the father or fathers of her children? Does it matter that she says nothing about them? Or are there clues as to who he/they might be?

8. Is Sila's life ever open to something other than grief and rage?

9. What kind of humor does Sila have?

10. How does the novel dramatize what is happening at this moment in South Africa's early history? What are the differences and conflicts between the English and the Dutch that filter through Sila's story?

11. Do you perceive any differences between what you know of slavery in, say, the Americas, and the world that unfolds in Sila's story?

12. Why would we be interested in yet another slave story? What does this book have to say that is different?

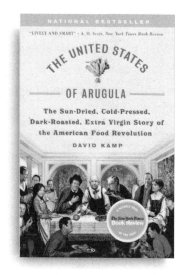

THE UNITED STATES OF ARUGULA

The Sun-Dried, Cold-Pressed, Dark-Roasted, Extra Virgin Story of the American Food Revolution

AUTHOR: *David Kamp*

PUBLISHER: Broadway Books, July 2007

WEBSITE: www.davidkamp.com
www.broadwaybooks.com

AVAILABLE IN:
Paperback, 416 pages, $14.95
ISBN: 978-0-7679-1580-9

SUBJECT: American History/Culture (Nonfiction)

"A page-turner filled with fascinating footnotes, a delicious dish about bold-faced names, and an in-depth look at the ways in which a series of food pioneers touched off a revolution." —USA Today

"Culturally aware and cleverly written, this anatomy of the French-fried versus sun-dried tension at the heart of American gastronomy is refreshingly non-snooty." —Atlantic Monthly

*"With the sweep of an epic novel, David Kamp takes us behind the scenes and into the sweaty, wacky, weird trenches of the Great American Food Revolution. His reporting is solid, his storytelling magnificent, and his good humor is seemingly inexhaustible. . . . A terrific book." —**Molly O'Neill***

Summary: The United States of Arugula is the story of an American revolution—the dramatic culinary changes that brought robust international flavors to a table formerly piled high with bland meat and potatoes.

A thrilling ride through decades of innovation and food politics, *The United States of Arugula* delivers a wickedly entertaining history of these cultural changes. Brimming with insider details and rarely reported anecdotes, this is a cultural history any book club can savor.

ABOUT THE AUTHOR: **David Kamp** has been a writer and editor for *Vanity Fair* and *GQ* for more than a decade, specializing in writing about the arts. He lives in New York with his wife and two children.

1. What are your best and worst childhood memories of food? Are your eating habits better or worse than those of your parents? Which of the transformations described in *The United States of Arugula* has been most relevant in your lifetime?

2. What aspects of the Big Three—James Beard, Julia Child, and Craig Claiborne—made them unlikely figures in launching America's culinary revolution?

3. What discoveries did you make about early American cookery, and the palates of nineteenth–century Americans? What does the history of a nation's food indicate about the history of its populations?

4. What is distinctly American about the success of smaller venues that grew to have broad appeal—such as Dean & DeLuca, or ice cream shops like Steve's or Ben & Jerry's? Can such companies grow infinitely without reducing quality and without giving frontline employees an unfair deal?

5. Discuss the ways the food revolution has led to markets for products besides food, such as the wares sold in stores like Williams–Sonoma, or the craze to remodel kitchens with restaurant-quality appliances. To what extent does quality home cooking truly rely on tools of the trade?

6. What did America's early resistance to ethnic cuisine say about American society? What international flavors proliferate in your community? Can you trace their arrival, and the way such restaurants were initially received?

7. Why do you suppose the history of America's culinary transformations volley from the East Coast to the West Coast, with Charlie Trotter in Chicago as a rare Midwest voice? What is it about these two coastal populations that placed them at the forefront of change? Do they have a monopoly on the food world's palate?

8. What has been the effect of television in changing the way we understand culinary trends? What is your reaction to cooking shows?

9. Do national chains such as Starbuck's and Whole Foods make it easier or harder for independent food start–ups to thrive? Has their presence had any impact on your cravings, or on the way you shop?

10. What class wars seemed to be simmering behind the transitions described in *The United States of Arugula*? What aspects of the story demonstrate the power of the elite, and which aspects are populist? What separates the arugula consumers from the fans of iceberg lettuce?

THE VANISHING POINT

AUTHOR: *Mary Sharratt*

PUBLISHER: Mariner Books, June 2006

WEBSITE: www.marinerbooks.com
www.marysharratt.com

AVAILABLE IN:
Paperback, 385 pages, $12.95
ISBN: (13) 978-0-618-46233-9
ISBN: (10) 0-618-46233-3

SUBJECT: American History/Women's
Lives/Personal Challenges (Fiction)

"A truly captivating novel. It wears its history lightly, in the best tradition of great historical fiction. Mary Sharratt has a marvelously deft touch. . . . She keeps the reader completely engaged, from first page to last."
— **Katharine Weber, author of** *The Little Women*

SUMMARY: Bright and inquisitive, Hannah Powers was raised by a father who treated her as if she were his son by giving her a forbidden education. While her beautiful and reckless sister, May, pushes the limits of propriety in their small English town. But Hannah's secret serves her well when she journeys to colonial Maryland to reunite with May, who has been married off to a distant cousin after her sexual misadventures ruined her marriage prospects in England.

As Hannah searches for May in Maryland, who has disappeared, she is freed from the constraints of the society that judged both her and May as dangerous—too smart, too fearless, and too hungry for life. But Hannah is also plagued by doubt, as her quest for answers to May's fate grows ever more disturbing and tangled.

This is tale of dark suspense, love, and betrayal—two sisters, one lost and the other searching.

ABOUT THE AUTHOR: **Mary Sharratt** spent ten years of research for *The Vanishing Point*. She is also the author of the novels *Summit Avenue*, which was selected as a Book Sense Pick, and *The Real Minerva*, a winner of the Willa Literary Award and a finalist for the Minnesota Book Award. Sharratt lives in Lancashire, England.

1. While May often spent her time in the care of Joan, the housekeeper, Hannah was educated by her physician father, despite laws that forbade women from studying medicine. Why do you suppose the sisters were raised so differently? What prompted Dr. Powers to train his younger daughter in the sciences?

2. Do you agree that the arranged marriage is the best solution to May's problems? Would you have reacted as May does when she realizes that she and her only sister will be separated by an ocean? Do you believe that May, on leaving England, truly expects to see Hannah again?

3. How might the sisters lives have been different if they had been born at another time? Which sister was better equipped to handle life in the New World?

4. Mary Sharratt's fascinating descriptions of social customs, recipes, and medical practices are woven throughout the novel; how do they add to your understanding of Hannah's world?

5. After a long, lonely journey from England to America, Hannah arrives at the Washbrook Plantation only to discover that her sister is missing. Why does Hannah stay on the estate? Would you have stayed? How is Hannah's life in Maryland governed by May's absence?

6. As you learn more about May's marriage to Gabriel, what do you think of their pairing? Does this knowledge have any bearing on the way you view Hannah's relationship with Gabriel?

7. If *The Vanishing Point* is a story of love and betrayal, who commits the ultimate betrayal—and against whom? What relationship marks the emotional center of the book for you—the relationship between Hannah and May, or between Hannah and Gabriel?

8. As the only women on their wilderness homestead, May and Adele forge a tight bond that transcends class and race. Does Adele eventually usurp Hannah's place in May's heart? Who ultimately shows May the greatest love and loyalty—Adele or Hannah?

9. Given what you know of life in the colonies—its moral codes, double standards, and hardships—do you think Gabriel and Hannah are at an advantage or a disadvantage living so far away from society?

10. Does Hannah finally achieve her full potential in pursuing an independent life, or does she betray her own heart?

11. What do you think about the revelations at the end of the book? Which character—Hannah, May, Gabriel, or Adele—comes closest to achieving an independent, self-governed life in America?

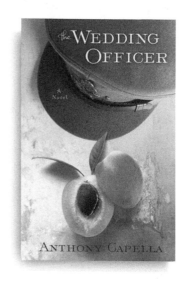

THE WEDDING OFFICER

AUTHOR: *Anthony Capella*

PUBLISHER: Bantam, May 2007

WEBSITE: www.bantamdell.com
www.theweddingofficer.com

AVAILABLE IN:
Hardcover, 448 pages, $22.00
ISBN: (13) 978-0-553-80547-5
ISBN: (10) 0-553-80547-9

SUBJECT: Relationships/History/
Culture & World Issues (Fiction)

"Capella again mingles amore with alimenti in this tale of a British officer who develops an appetite for all things Italian. . . . [The author's] prose becomes transcendent when he pours his heart into telling the story of Italian food." —**Kirkus Reviews**

"Food, Italy, and romance are Anthony Capella's trademark topics. He combines all three deliciously in The Wedding Officer.*"* —**InStyle**

SUMMARY: In the sumptuous tradition of *Chocolat* and *Captain Corelli's Mandolin*, and already optioned for a major motion picture, comes a magical tale of romantic passion, culinary delight—and Italy.

Captain James Gould arrives in wartime Naples assigned to discourage marriages between British soldiers and their gorgeous Italian girlfriends. But the innocent young officer is soon distracted by an intoxicating young widow who knows her way around a kitchen. Livia Pertini is creating feasts that stun the senses with their succulence—ruby-colored San Marzana tomatoes, glistening anchovies, and delectable new potatoes encrusted with the black volcanic earth of of Campania—and James is about to learn that his heart may rank higher than his orders. For romance can be born of the sweet and spicy passions of food and love—and time spent in the kitchen can be as joyful and exciting as the banquet of life itself!

ABOUT THE AUTHOR: **Anthony Capella** is an author, self-proclaimed Italophile, and lover of all things culinary. He lives in Oxfordshire with his wife and three children. His first novel, *The Food of Love*, is being made into a film by DiNovi Pictures.

1. What aspects of Livia's personality are illustrated in the novel's opening scenes? What parts of her identity fade after Enzo leaves, and what aspects are intensified when she is on her own?

2. Discuss the different types of hunger described in *The Wedding Officer*. Which ones are the most powerful—the hunger for companionship, food, or sex? In what way do James's and Livia's appetites change throughout the novel?

3. Why did James's superiors believe it was necessary to regulate the marriages between servicemen and their Italian girlfriends? What did the interview questions indicate about the gulf between reality and pretense during this episode in history?

4. Discuss the issue of language as it plays out in the novel. How does it help and hinder the characters to have limitations in their ability to communicate? In what ways is food a universal language? What did James's "food language," which forbade things like garlic and emphasized potatoes over pasta, say about his personality?

5. Livia highlights the sensual pleasures of food when she serves the officers snails and peas, all still in their shells. What other ways does she have of using food to seduce?

6. How familiar were you with Italy's experience with the war, and the rise of Mussolini? What aspects of history and culture in *The Wedding Officer* surprised you?

7. How did the economics of war become a sort of weapon as well? Was James right to try to eliminate the black market? How does corruption become defined under these circumstances? Beyond the issue of nutrition, what does it do to a community to deprive them of their national cuisine?

8. In chapter thirty, James is exasperated to discover that Livia doesn't measure any of her ingredients. What turning points does this scene capture? What do they eventually teach each other about intuition and rules?

9. Livia deeply resents the Allies. What does her story demonstrate about the role of liberators in a foreign land?

10. Would you have given in to Alberto's demands if you had been in Livia's position? Was the survival of her family always the top priority in her life?

11. Livia tells James she is adamant in her support of communism. What aspects of history are captured in this conversation? What makes communism so appealing to her? What is her understanding of its promise?

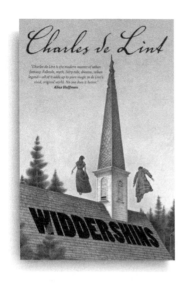

WIDDERSHINS

AUTHOR: *Charles de Lint*

PUBLISHER: Tor Books, June 2007

WEBSITE: www.tor.com
www.sfsite.com/charlesdelint

AVAILABLE IN:
Paperback, 560 pages, $14.95

ISBN: (13) 978-0-7653-1286-0
ISBN: (10) 0-7653-1286-7

SUBJECT: Fantasy/Relationships/
Personal Discovery (Fiction)

A June 2006 Book Sense Pick

"Charles de Lint is the modern master of urban fantasy. Folktale, myth, fairy tale, dreams, urban legend—all of it adds up to pure magic in de Lint's vivid, original world. No one does it better." —**Alice Hoffman**

". . . de Lint spins yet another magical story of the intersections between reality and the faerie and spirit world in this latest addition to the Newford opus, his twin loves of storytelling and music-making shining through every page. . . . [H]ighly recommended." —*Library Journal* (**starred review**)

SUMMARY: Jilly Coppercorn and Geordie Riddell. Since they were introduced in the first Newford story, "Timeskip," back in 1989, their friends and readers alike have been waiting for them to realize what everybody else already knows: that they belong together. Now in *Widdershins*, Jilly and Geordie's story is finally being told.

To walk "widdershins" is to walk counterclockwise or backwards around something. It's a classic pathway into the fairy realm. It's also the way people often back slowly into the relationships that matter, the real ones that make for a life.

ABOUT THE AUTHOR: **Charles de Lint** and his wife, the artist MaryAnn Harris, live in Ottawa, Ontario, Canada. His evocative novels, including *Moonheart, Forests of the Heart,* and *The Onion Girl,* have earned him a devoted following and critical acclaim as a master of contemporary magical fiction.

1. *Widdershins* is about a shadow world that exists, unseen, side by side with our own world. Lizzie stumbles into it one night when her car breaks down. How do the two worlds mirror one another? Does one seem better, or nobler? What elements of political and personal life occur in both realms, and how are they dealt with differently in each?

2. To know a being's true name, the author says, is to have power over that being. What is it about naming that carries so much weight? Do you think that the association between names and power is ever real in our world? If you had a true name distinct from your everyday "speaking name," what do you think it would be?

3. Jilly Coppercorn's story—both past and present—is about the separation between body and mind, and the final confrontation that she endures in *Widdershins* takes place when her physical self becomes trapped inside a pocket world created by her own mind. What is Jilly's final and most difficult task, in that world and in her life's story? How much power do our will, our beliefs, and our attitudes have over our physical health and wholeness? What kinds of roles can forgiveness play in it?

4. The conflict between Native North American populations and the descendants of the Europeans who displaced them is a fundamental theme in *Widdershins*. What characterizes each group? What do they cherish, and how do their respective value systems work? Are they irreconcilably different? Do they learn from one another at any point in the story?

5. Though hobbled by injury and traumatized in childhood, Jilly has never despaired—until she sees Geordie killed. How do people like her maintain hope and optimism when everything in life seems to weigh against them? To what degree are we victims of our circumstances and experiences? How much of a say do we have in the direction our lives take? What kinds of trauma is it possible to overcome, and what kinds mark the soul forever?

6. Only one of their deaths finally makes Jilly and Geordie realize that they can't live without one another. What has kept them from this knowledge for so long? Have you ever been able to learn or realize something crucial only in a moment of crisis? What happened to that knowledge once the crisis abated?

WITHOUT A MAP
A Memoir

AUTHOR: **Meredith Hall**

PUBLISHER: Beacon Press, May 2007

WEBSITE: www.meredithhall.org
www.beacon.org

AVAILABLE IN:
Hardcover, 248 pages, $24.95
ISBN: 978-080707273-8

SUBJECT: Family/Personal Challenges/
Women's Lives (Memoir)

"Written in spare, unsentimental prose, Without a Map *is stunning; Meredy's reunion with her grown son (who was raised in poverty with an abusive father) is the highlight. Book groups, take note."* —**Booklist**

"A haunting meditation on love, loss and family." —**Caroline Leavitt, People (4 stars)**

"An unusually powerful coming-of-age memoir. . . . Searching, humble and quietly triumphant: Hall has managed to avoid all the easy clichés." —**Kirkus**

SUMMARY: Meredith Hall's moving but unsentimental memoir begins in 1965, when she becomes pregnant at sixteen. Shunned by her insular New Hampshire community, she is then kicked out of the house by her mother. After giving her baby up for adoption, Hall wanders recklessly through the Middle East, where she survives by selling her possessions and finally her blood. She returns to New England and stitches together a life that encircles her silenced and invisible grief. When he is twenty-one, her lost son finds her. Their reunion is tender, turbulent, and ultimately redemptive. Hall's parents never ask for her forgiveness, yet as they age, she offers them her love. What sets *Without a Map* apart is the way in which loss and betrayal evolve into compassion, and compassion into wisdom.

ABOUT THE AUTHOR: **Meredith Hall** graduated from Bowdoin College at the age of forty-four. Her work has appeared in the *The New York Times*, *Creative Nonfiction*, *The Southern Review*, *Five Points*, *Prairie Schooner*, and several anthologies. She teaches writing at the University of New Hampshire and lives in Maine.

1. Relationships form some of Meredith's central challenges: relationships with her mother, her father, Catherine, Erik, Paul, Ruth, Armi, William. What are some of the recurring challenges relationships provide? Do any of these relationships resemble your own challenges with relationships?

2. When Meredith calls her mother from High Mowing School, looking for sympathy, her mother tells her. "You have no choice. You'll be fine. . . . You are a survivor." What would you have told Meredith? How does Meredith eventually survive and flourish?

3. What roles do you think the wilderness and domestication play in the unfolding drama of Meredith's life? Do they have roles in your life?

4. *Without a Map* continually makes reference to the political activities of the 60s—the Hampton Beach riots, the Vietnam War, demonstrations in Cambridge. Yet the narrator says that she doesn't consider what happened to her to be a product of the times. Do you think the setting in time is important? Could this be a story of anytime?

5. The sense of belonging is continually interrupted by losses in Meredith's life, but Meredith finally concludes, "I will return home, part of the world." What is home, and what does it mean to belong?

6. Chapter Thirteen ends with the words, "We love each other. We need each other. That is our only map." How is love a map? Is love a map in your life?

7. Why were other misfits tolerated, but not the pregnant girl? As young people, Paul stands up to Armi, but Meredith didn't stand up to her father or to her mother. Do you think this has anything to do with gender roles? Are middle-aged women invisible? Is Meredith invisible?

8. We meet many mothers in *Without a Map*: Meredith's mother, Meredith, Catherine, Ruth, the girl who comes to the photocopy shop, the women in the desert. What does *Without a Map* say about being a mother?

9. Does forgiveness always require words? Is anything lacking in the forgiveness Meredith and her mother offer each other? What about Meredith and her father, Meredith and Paul, Ruth and Paul and Armi?

10. The latter chapters refer often to death: the death of Meredith's mother, of Ruth, of William, the impending death of Meredith's father. Do you think thoughts about death contribute in any way to the sense of calm that pervades the last chapter?

This guide was created by
Mary Johnson of A Room Of Her Own Foundation

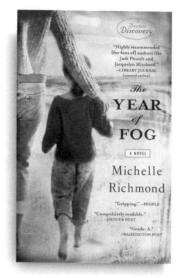

THE YEAR OF FOG

AUTHOR: *Michelle Richmond*

PUBLISHER: Bantam Discovery, March 2008

WEBSITE: www.bantamdell.com
www.michellerichmond.com

AVAILABLE IN:
Paperback, 416 pages, $12.00
ISBN: (13) 978-0-385-34012-0
ISBN: (10) 0-385-34012-5

SUBJECT: Intrigue/Family/Relationships (Fiction)

"Richmond gracefully explores the nature of memory and perception in key passages that never slow the suspense of the search. Closely echoing Jacquelyn Mitchard's best-selling Deep End of the Ocean *(1996), this is a page-turner with a philosophical bent."* —**Booklist**

"A spare page-turner . . . beautifully paced . . . the book's twist on missing child stories is wholly effective." —**Publishers Weekly**

"Involving, heart-rending and immediately readable...Richmond captures the spirit of life in The City." —**The San Francisco Examiner**

"A mesmerizing novel of loss and grief, hope and redemption, and the endurance of love." —**Library Journal** (starred review)

SUMMARY: Life changes in an instant. While walking on the beach with Emma, her fiancé's six-year old daughter, photographer Abby Mason commits her greatest error. In the seconds she turns to look into her camera, Emma disappears in the thick San Francisco fog. Heartbreaking, uplifting, and beautifully told, here is the riveting tale of a family torn apart, of the search for the truth behind a child's disappearance, and of one woman's unwavering faith in the redemptive power of love.

ABOUT THE AUTHOR: **Michelle Richmond** is the author of the novel *Dream of the Blue Room* and a story collection which won the Associated Writing Programs Award. She is also the recipient of the 2006 Mississippi Review Prize. Michelle lives with her husband and son in San Francisco.

1. *The Year of Fog* unfolds as a series of flashbacks and present-tense scenes. How do Abby's impressions of her own past shift as she searches for Emma? What does her research on the neuroscience of memory tell us about the limits and the power of the mind's imagery?

2. How much was Emma a factor in Abby's relationship with Jake? After Emma's disappearance, what did they discover about each other? Why was it awkward for Abby to see Jake turn to religion? Why was he skeptical of her insistence that Emma didn't drown but was kidnapped?

3. How does Abby's eye as a photographer shape the way she sees the world around her? What does she see that others don't? What does her approach to photography indicate about her approach to life?

4. How did Abby's recollections of her own mother affect her approach to being a stepmother?

5. Describing the ancient history of memory studies in chapter 43, Abby mentions the concept of Renaissance "memory theaters" and later has a dream in which her memories are displayed in ways she cannot fully comprehend. If your past were to be categorized in such a way, what would it look like? Which objects would best represent various events? Which of your memories would you most like to preserve?

6. Abby struggles with feelings of inadequacy, seeing herself as the sister who often botches her chances at a happier life. What accounts for the tremendous differences between her self-perception and Annabel's?

7. For Abby, one of the most difficult aspects of the search is the fact that she doesn't receive full respect as a key figure in Emma's life. Ultimately, how do you define "a devoted mother"? What are the best examples of good parenting in the novel? What determines whether someone has what it takes to be a good parent?

8. What enabled Abby to uncover the truth while Jake could not? Was it her intuition? Determination? Hypnosis? Fate? Or simply the deep guilt she felt? What ultimately caused the fog to lift in Emma's disappearance?

9. In many ways, the novel is a poignant portrait of coping with grief, in this case a very unresolved form of grief. What is the best way to confront tragedy?

10. As you saw Abby catch a wave in the final paragraph, what did you predict for her future?

READ THE CLASSICS

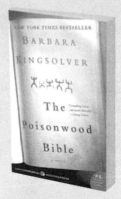

 book club girl

Visit our blog at www.BookClubGirl.com.
Dedicated to sharing great books, news,
and tips with book club girls everywhere.

HARPER PERENNIAL   Read our blog at www.OliveReader.com

Visit the **VP BOOK CLUB**
to enhance your
READING GROUP EXPERIENCE

vpbookclub.com

VIKING

Members of Penguin Group (USA)

PENGUIN
BOOKS

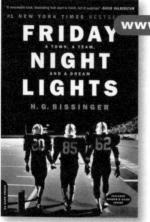

GREAT CLASSICS

make great reading group choices

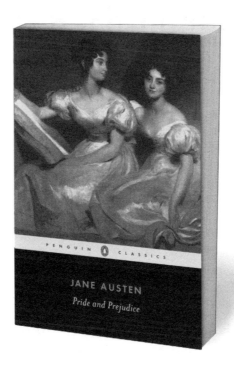

www.penguinclassics.com

www.vpbookclub.com

Penguin Classics
A member of Penguin Group (USA)

Lady Banks'
Commonplace Book

*a newsletter for people who love Southern Literature
(and literary gossip)*

Book Reviews from Southern Booksellers

Author Readings & Book Signings

Book Festivals & Literary Events

Literary News & Gossip

Interviews

Essays & Commentary

Excerpts in Excellent Literary Taste
(as selected by Her ladyship, the editor)

*subscribe now at ladybanks@sibaweb.com
also available at*

authorsroundthesouth.com

Selecting Discussible Books Since 1995

Reading Group Choices' goal is to join with publishers, bookstores, libraries, trade associations, and authors to develop resources to enhance the reading group experience.

Reading Group Choices is distributed annually to bookstores, libraries, and directly to book groups. Titles from previous issues are posted on the **www.ReadingGroupChoices.com** website. Books presented here have been recommended by book group members, librarians, booksellers, literary agents, publicists, authors, and publishers. All submissions are then reviewed to ensure the discussibility of each title. Once a title is approved for inclusion by the Advisory Board (see below), publishers are asked to underwrite production costs, so that copies of *Reading Group Choices* can be distributed for a minimal charge.

For additional copies, please call your local library or bookstore, or contact us by phone or email as shown below. Quantities are limited. For more information, please visit our website at **www.ReadingGroupChoices.com**

Toll-free: 1-866-643-6883 • info@ReadingGroupChoices.com

READING GROUP CHOICES' ADVISORY BOARD

Donna Paz Kaufman founded the bookstore training and consulting group of Paz & Associates in 1992, with the objective of creating products and services to help independent bookstores and public libraries remain viable in today's market. A few years later, she met and married **Mark Kaufman**, whose background included project management, marketing communications, and human resources. Together, they launched **Reading Group Choices** in 1995 to bring publishers, booksellers, libraries, and readers closer together. They sold **Reading Group Choices** to Barbara and Charlie Mead in May 2005. They now offer training and education for new and prospective booksellers, architectural design services for bookstores and libraries, marketing support through *The Reader's Edge* customer newsletter, and some print and video products on a wide variety of topics. To learn more about Paz & Associates, visit www.pazbookbiz.com.

John Mutter is editor-in-chief of *Shelf Awareness*, the daily e-mail newsletter focusing on books, media about books, retailing and related issues to help booksellers, librarians and others do their jobs more effectively.

Before he and his business partner, Jenn Risko, founded the company in May 2005, he was executive editor of bookselling at *Publishers Weekly*. He has covered book industry issues for 25 years and written for a variety of publications, including *The Bookseller* in the U.K.; *Australian Bookseller & Publisher*; *Boersenblatt*, the German book trade magazine; and *College Store Magazine* in the U.S. For more information about *Shelf Awareness*, go to its Web site, www.shelf-awareness.com.

Nancy Olson has owned and operated Quail Ridge Books & Music in Raleigh, NC, since 1984, which has grown from 1,200 sq. ft. to 9,000+ sq. ft and sales of $3.2 million. The bookstore won three major awards in 2001: *Publishers Weekly* Bookseller of the Year, Charles Haslam Award for Excellence in Bookselling; Pannell Award for Excellence in Children's Bookselling. It was voted "Best in the Triangle" in the *Independent Weekly* and *Metro Magazine*.

Mark Nichols was an independent bookseller in various locations from Maine to Connecticut from 1976 through 1993. After seven years in a variety of positions with major publishers in New York and San Francisco, he joined the American Booksellers Association in 2000, and currently serves as the Director of Book Sense Marketing. He is also on the Board of the Small Press Center, and has edited two volumes with Newmarket Press—*Book Sense Best Books* (2004) and *Book Sense Best Children's Books* (2005).

RESOURCES

THE INTERNET

About reading groups and book clubs

- **ReadingGroupChoices.com**—Over 600 guides available plus give-aways and fun and interactive materials for reading groups.

- **bookgroupexpo.com**— Come to book group expo and celebrate.

- **Book-Clubs-Resource.com**—A guide to book clubs and reading groups with a collection of links and information for readers, including information about saving with discount book clubs.

- **BookClubCookbook.com**—Recipes and food for thought from your book club's favorite books and authors

About Books

- **ShelfAwareness.com**—A free e-mail newsletter dedicated to helping the people in stores, in libraries and on the Web buy, sell, and lend books most wisely.

- **PageByPageBooks.com**—Read classic books online for free.

- **PublishingInsidertypad.com**—Books, music, movies, the big picture, and absurd rants.

- **GenerousBooks.com**—A community for those who love books and love to discuss them

- **BookMuse.com**— Commentary, author bios, and suggestions for further reading

- **BookBrowse.com**— Book reviews, excerpts, and author interviews

- **AverageReader.com**—Book reviews - honest and to the point

- **BookSpot.com**—Help in your search for the best book-related content on the Web

■ **Publisher Web Sites**—Find additional topics for discussion, special offers for book groups, and other titles of interest.

Algonquin Books of Chapel Hill—**algonquin.com**

Anchor Books—**readinggroupcenter.com**

Ballantine Books—**ballantinebooks.com/BRC**

Bantam Dell—**bantamdell.com**

Beacon Press—**beacon.org**

Broadway Books—**broadwaybooks.com**

Conari Press—**conari.com**

DaCapo Press—**dacapopress.com**

Dial Press—**dialpress.com**

Doubleday—**doubleday.com**

Feminist Press at C.U.N.Y.—**feministpress.org**

Harper Paperbacks—**harpercollins.com**

Harper Perennial—**harperperennial.com**

Hyperion—**hyperionbooks.com**

Mariner Books—**marinerbooks.com**

MacAdam/Cage—**macadamcage.com**

Middleway Press—**middlewaypress.com**

Nan. A. Talese—**nanatalese.com**

Other Press—**otherpress.com**

Penguin Books—**penguin.com**

Picador USA—**picadorusa.com**

Plume—**penguin.com**

PublicAffairs—**publicaffairsbooks.com**

Random House—**randomhouse.com**

Soho Press—**sohopress.com**

St. Martin's Griffin — **stmartins.com**

Toby Press—**tobypress.com**

Tor—**tor.com**

Unbridled Books—**unbridledbooks.com**

Vintage Books—**readinggroupcenter.com**

W. W. Norton—**wwnorton.com**

BOOKS

■ *Book Lust: Recommended Reading for Every Mood, Moment, and Reason* by Nancy Pearl
Published by Sasquatch Books, ISBN 1-57061-381-8, $16.95.

■ *More Book Lust: Recommended Reading for Every Mood, Moment, and Reason* by Nancy Pearl
Published by Sasquatch Books, ISBN 1-57061-435-0 $16.95.

■ *The Book Club Companion: A Comprehensive Guide to the Reading Group Experience* by Diana Loevy
Published by Berkeley Books, ISBN 0-425-21009-X, $14.00.

■ *The Book Club Cookbook: Recipes and Food for Thought from Your Book Club's Favorite Books and Authors* by Judy Gelman and Vicki Levy Krupp
Published by Tarcher/Penguin, ISBN 1-58542-322-X, $15.95.

■ *The Book Group Book: A Thoughtful Guide to Forming and Enjoying a Stimulating Book Discussion Group.* Edited by Ellen Slezak and Margaret Eleanor Atwood
Published by Chicago Review Press, ISBN 1-5565-2412-9, $14.95.

■ *Circles of Sisterhood: A Book Discussion Group Guide for Women of Color* by Pat Neblett
Published by Writers & Readers, ISBN 0-8631-6245-2, $14.

■ *Family Book Sharing Groups: Start One in Your Neighborhood!* by Marjorie R. Simic with Eleanor C. MacFarlane
Published by the Family Literacy Center
ISBN 1-8837-9011-5, $6.95.

■ *Good Books Lately: The One-Stop Resource for Book Groups and Other Greedy Readers* by Ellen Moore and Kira Stevens
Published by St. Martin's Griffin, ISBN 978-0-312-30961-9, $13.95.

■ *Leave Me Alone, I'm Reading: Finding and Losing Myself in Books* by Maureen Corrigan
Published by Random House, ISBN 0-375-50425-7, $24.95.

- *Literature Circles: Voice and Choice in Book Clubs and Reading Groups* by Harvey Daniels
  Published by Stenhouse Publishers
  ISBN 1-5711-0333-3, $22.50.

- *The Mother-Daughter Book Club: How Ten Busy Mothers and Daughters Came Together to Talk, Laugh and Learn Through Their Love of Reading* by Shireen Dodson and Teresa Barker
  Published by HarperCollins, ISBN 0-0609-5242-3, $14.

- *Running Book Discussion Groups* by Lauren Zina John
  Published by Neal-Schuman, ISBN 1-55570-542-1.

- *The Reading Group Handbook: Everything You Need to Know to Start Your Own Book Club* by Rachel Jacobsohn
  Published by Hyperion, ISBN 0-786-88324-3, $12.95.

- *Recipe for a Book Club: A Monthly Guide for Hosting Your Own Reading Group: Menus & Recipes, Featured Authors, Suggested Readings, and Topical Questions* by Mary O'Hare and Rose Storey
  Published by Capital Books, ISBN 978-1-931-86883-9, $19.95

- *Talking About Books: Literature Discussion Groups in K–8 Classrooms* by Kathy Short
  Published by Heinemann, ISBN 0-3250-0073-5, $24.

- *Thirteen Ways of Looking at the Novel* by Jane Smiley Published by Knopf, ISBN 1-4000-4059-0, $26.95.

- *What to Read: The Essential Guide for Reading Group Members and Other Book Lovers (Revised)* by Mickey Pearlman
  Published by HarperCollins, ISBN 0-0609-5313-6, $14.00.

- *A Year of Reading: A Month-By-Month Guide to Classics and Crowd-Pleasers for You or Your Book Group* by H. E. Ellington and Jane Freimiller
  Published by Sourcebooks, ISBN 1-5707-1935-7, $14.95.

READING GROUP Choices

We wish to thank the authors, agents, publicists, librarians, booksellers, and our publishing colleagues who have continued to support this publication by calling to our attention some quality books for group discussion, and the publishers and friends who have helped to underwrite this edition.

Algonquin Books
of Chapel Hill

Anchor Books

Ballantine Books

Bantam

Bantam Discovery

Beacon Press

Broadway Books

Conari Press

DaCapo Press

Dial Press

Doubleday

Feminist Press at CUNY

Harper Paperbacks

Harper Perennial

Hyperion

MacAdam/Cage

Mariner Books

Middleway Press

Nan A. Talese

Other Press

Penguin Books

Picador USA

Plume

PublicAffairs

Soho Press

Southern Independent
Booksellers Alliance (SIBA)

St. Martin's Griffin

Toby Press

Tor

Unbridled Books

Vintage Books

W. W. Norton

Tips for Starting a Reading Group
An Exclusive by *Reading Group Choices*

Thinking about starting a *book group*? The process can begin by simply asking some people you know to help you organize the first gathering. Address the following questions early on to create a book group that is well run, interesting, and rewarding.

Group Composition
- What's the ideal size of the group?
- If you need to recruit members, how will you extend invitations?
- What requirements do you have for membership?

Reading Preferences
- What types of books will you read?
- Will you focus your reading to specific topics or genres?

Selection Process
- How will you choose which books to read?
- How far ahead will you plan?
- How will members obtain copies of books?

Meeting Logistics
- Where will you meet?
- How often?
- Will you meet in the same location each time or rotate your meeting locations?
- How long will meetings last?
- Will refreshments be provided?
- By whom?
- What time will be designated specifically for socializing?

Facilitating Discussion
- How will each discussion be lead?
- Will you designate a leader?
- Who is responsible for providing author information and giving an introduction to the group's discussion?
- What ground rules should be established?
- Can members who haven't read the book attend?
- Will guest speakers be invited?

Preparing for Your Next Discussion

An Exclusive by *Reading Group Choices*

Thanks to the many reading groups who have sent us your suggestions about making your discussions lively and interesting. We heard one thing loud and clear from many of you—*a little preparation goes a long way*! According to our recent survey,* the group leader/facilitator and/or the members engage in some preparation in nearly 90% of book groups. Hopefully, some of the ideas below gleaned from your colleagues' experiences will help you to make your discussions lively and fun.

PREPARATION IMPROVES DISCUSSION

1. Research reviews and background for "gems" to enliven discussions

2. Know your author

3. Choose *discussible* books

4. Prepare food & drink

One suggestion from a book group member: a discussion leader's "'homework' can often provide little 'gems' of information that can keep the discussion lively, spice it up or just plain keep it moving."

Another: "We always research the authors and books. Sometimes if there is something different about the book, we'll add it to the discussion. We learned about Mah Jong when we read *The Joy Luck Club*."

Still another: "We have found that it is necessary for at least one person to have read the book before recommending it for discussion. Some books are good to read, but not discussible."

Even bestselling author **Barbara Delinsky** rang in on this topic. "My group has a rule that a member can only recommend a book she has read, rather than pass on a second-hand recommendation—because each book group is different, with different makeup, different needs, different pacing, different types of discussions. We want to read books that will inspire lively discussion in our own group," she says.

Several of you prepared food and drink to accompany the discussion. One of you stated, "something light (especially if related in some way to the title or author) can make things a bit more fun."

---

*The statistics and suggestions herein are the results of **Reading Group Choices**' survey of thousands of book group members conducted in early 2007.

Choosing Discussible Books

An Exclusive by *Reading Group Choices*

What's the best way for your group to pick its next read? Many groups strive for consensus in advance about the *kind* of books they plan to read. Many even use formal (or not-so-formal) voting processes to make their selections. Some groups set aside one meeting to create a list or theme for the coming year. Lots of groups require that members follow guidelines when suggesting books for discussion. Readers have given us all kinds of ideas*—maybe some of them will work for your group!

Selection Methods

Getting consensus can be difficult, but most groups feel that it is important to do so. The majority of groups in our recent survey said that the group chooses books together. In many other groups, a single member chooses for each discussion, but every member has a chance to make a selection for the group. Most groups have established some kind of process for choosing discussible titles.

We found that many groups use some variation of a **rotation method**, in which one member suggests a number of titles at each meeting, and the group votes to make the final pick. A couple of intricate, but time-tested, variations of this method are described on the *Reading Group Choices* website.

Many other groups use a variation on the **bean method**. Here, each member brings 6 books that they suggest for discussion to a group gathering, and the books are laid out on the table. Each member is then given 50 beans. The members "vote" on the books they would like to discuss by placing as many beans as they want on the books they want to discuss. (The more beans they place, the more they would like to discuss that book.) In the words of one group, "The result is a valuable weighted list to choose from that lasts for a good long while!"

Several groups use **selection committees** to make the final selection. One group says, "At our season wrap-up, members present their recommendations for the next year based on their research or recommendations from other sources. A selection committee evaluates the recommendations and selects the books for the following year."

Lead Time

Nearly half of the groups in our survey choose their reading list for the entire year (or for several months) in advance at one meeting, and they

---

BOOK SELECTION METHODS

1. *Rotation:* Different member suggests selections each month.

2. *Voting:* Use beans to rank book selections.

3. *Committee:* Selection committee suggests "shortlist" or makes final choice.

---

usually use one of the selection methods described above. The most popular months for book selection were January and September.

Some groups, though, have a *rolling* advance list of the books they will discuss. Says one group, "Everyone picks a month, and has to wait to announce the selection. October is announced at the April meeting, November at the May meeting, and so on. That allows six months to find and read books, and the 'Book Chooser' can get a feel for the kinds of books the group has been reading. That way, the new choices compliment what the group has been reading, and no one will have bought a year's worth of books and be mad if someone changes their mind (which had been a problem). It is a nice surprise each month to hear what is coming up!"

Rules and Tools

Over half of the groups in our survey have adopted some procedures or rules about how discussions take place, and some of them apply to how books are selected.

Many groups require that the member recommending a book must have read it and be willing to read it again. Some groups insist that the book be available in paperback, or at least, readily available from local stores and/or libraries.

SUCCESSFUL SELECTION RULES AND TOOLS

1. *Read in Advance:* Person suggesting book must have read it.

2. *Variety:* Choose several genres and subject areas to discuss.

3. *Proven Choices:* Use "Top-10" discussible book list for selection ideas.

Many groups agree that they want to "stretch their horizons" by reading a variety of genres and subject material during the course of the year, and they establish processes to help achieve that goal. For example, one group stipulates that "1) Chosen books must be discussible, and 2) You don't have to like them." Groups have found that they need to be careful here, though. In the words of one group, "the challenge has been choosing a book that doesn't offend the sensitivities of recent personal situations within the book (i.e. breast cancer, death of a parent or spouse, divorce, etc.) Sometimes it is hard to come up with a book that stays clear of the issues involved!"

Of course, many groups choose titles from the selections in the *Reading Group Choices* print edition or on the website, and some refer to the "Top 10 Discussible Books" from the annual *Reading Group Choices* survey of book club members.

---

*The statistics and suggestions herein are the results of **Reading Group Choices'** survey of thousands of book group members conducted in early 2007.

Handling "Book Group Divas"

An Exclusive by *Reading Group Choices*

Our recent survey revealed that almost two-thirds of reading groups have had a group member dominate a discussion and prevent others from speaking at some time. Some of them just let it pass, and the problem did not persist. But the rest found it necessary to take some action so that everyone in the group could have fun and take part in the discussions. Many groups have asked to hear what others groups did about their "Book Group Divas," so we've summarized your comments here. Thanks to all who provided us with the benefit of their experience.

Many groups found that advance preparations helped prevent such a problem from occurring in the first place. Establishing guidelines such as, "Everyone gets a chance to talk," "Only one person talks at a time," "No side conversations," helped to set the tone for future discussions. Some groups have even established a time limit for any one member to speak about a single topic.

Having a list of discussion questions ready for each gathering also helped, because it made redirecting the discussion easier. Some groups that had never established guidelines before simply made an announcement to the group (including the "diva") that everybody had something to say and needs a turn to speak. Some even established a new convention that rotated the discussion among each and every member to ensure that everyone had a chance to speak.

Many of you reported that the task fell to the discussion leader, who gently and politely redirected the discussion back to the book, to the next discussion question, or to another group member. (In a few cases, the "redirection" was not so gentle or polite, resulting in the "diva's" leaving the group!)

> **6 WAYS TO HANDLE "DIVAS"**
>
> 1. Establish guidelines in advance.
>
> 2. Have discussion questions ready.
>
> 3. "Redirect" discussion.
>
> 4. Confront diva (privately or during discussion).
>
> 5. Get consensus before admitting new members. Don't let potential "divas" join.
>
> 6. Disband and form new group(s).

Groups without a formal leader spoke with the "diva" privately or took turns bringing the discussion around to others. Comments like, "Excuse me, Susie—I'm having difficulty hearing Jane," or just plain "Shhhhh," seemed to work well in some cases. In groups where the members have established strong relationships, a member might say, "You've had your say, and now it's my turn!" without ruffling too many feathers.

In a few cases, the problem actually caused the group to disband. In those cases, group members in their new groups are careful about inviting new members to join. In some cases, the group votes before a new member is invited.

The problem is definitely a thorny one. Hopefully, some of the ideas that your colleagues have used will help you to keep your discussions fun and lively.

Ice-Breakers

An *Exclusive* by *Reading Group Choices*

Do you need an ice-breaker for a new reading group? What will you do for your book selection month or holiday party? How about something to add more excitement to one of your meetings? The answer: play a game—and not the cheesy bridal shower games, but *Book Group Games*! These games are perfect to get to know new members and find out something more about veteran members!

Favorite Book. Every member brings their favorite book in a bag with their name in the bag. Everyone hands their bag to the hostess/host/leader (h/h/l). He/She will be the only one who knows who brought which book. (If you don't have your favorite book—write the title of a piece of paper.) The h/h/l writes down the members names with their titles. Then, display all the books (or pieces of papers) on a table, and each member make a list trying to match the members and the books After everyone has completed their list, the h/h/l will announce each book and then poll the members to determine if anyone got the right person. Then, the person who brought the book reveals themselves. Continue on until all books are claimed.

Book Group Quiz. The h/h/l makes a little quiz and hands them out. Make the questions short and fun, and allow maybe 10 minutes for members to answer or at least make a guess. Then read the questions aloud, and have a ball sharing the answers.

Sample: Find member(s) who:
- Has read *War and Peace*.
- Has been in a book group before.
- Can explain the Dewey Decimal System.
- Has not read *Charlotte's Web*.
- Can recite a poem. Request they do so.
- Has written a poem or a short story.
- Can remember the name of their first grade teacher.
- Grew up using the bookmobile as their library.
- Knows the name of the protagonist in *Pride and Prejudice*.
- Can name the Seven Dwarfs.
- Has been to a book reading in the last six month.

And on and on! Be creative, and maybe create questions specific to your group. You can also put the questions on little scraps on paper, put them in a basket, and pass the basket.

Memory Game: Pick some books (5–7) and lay them on a tray for members to see and have them pass the tray around. Remove the tray and books from sight and have members list what titles were on the tray. The member that lists the most titles is the winner. You can give extra points or break ties by asking specific questions — like the author of three of the books—and so on. (*This game might require a little prize for the winner!*)

INDEX BY SUBJECT/INTEREST